15 Days of Prayer
With Pierre Teilhard de Chardin

Also in this collection:

André Gozier
15 Days of Prayer
With Thomas Merton

Michel Lafon
15 Days of Prayer
With Charles de Foucauld

Constant Tonnelier
15 Days of Prayer
With Saint Thérèse of Lisieux

François Vayne
15 Days of Prayer
With Saint Bernadette of Lourdes

15 DAYS OF PRAYER WITH

Pierre Teilhard de Chardin

ANDRÉ DUPLEIX

Translated by Victoria Hébert and Denis Sabourin

Liguori
LIGUORI, MISSOURI

Published by Liguori Publications
Liguori, Missouri
http://www.liguori.org

This book is a translation of *Prier 15 Jours Avec Pierre Teilhard de Chardin*, published by Nouvelle Cité, 1994, Montrouge, France.

Library of Congress Cataloging-in-Publication Data

Dupleix, André, 1944–
[Prier 15 jours avec Pierre Teilhard de Chardin. English]
15 days of prayer with Pierre Teilhard de Chardin / André Dupleix ; translated by Victoria Hébert and Denis Sabourin. — 1st English ed.
p. cm.
ISBN 0-7648-0490-1
1. Meditations. 2. Teilhard de Chardin, Pierre Meditations. 3. Spiritual life—Catholic Church. I. Title. II. Title: Fifteen days of prayer with Pierre Teilhard de Chardin.
BX2182.2.D8713 1999
269'.6—dc21 99-34433

Printed in the United States of America
03 02 01 00 99 5 4 3 2 1
First English Edition 1999

Table of Contents

How to Use This Book

AN OLD CHINESE PROVERB, or at least what I am able to recall of what is supposed to be an old Chinese proverb, goes something like this: "Even a journey of a thousand miles begins with a single step." When you think about it, the truth of the proverb is obvious. It is impossible to begin any project, let alone a journey, without taking the first step. I think it might also be true, although I cannot recall if another Chinese proverb says it, "that the first step is often the hardest." Or, as someone else once observed, "the distance between a thought and the corresponding action needed to implement the idea takes the most energy." I don't know who shared that perception with me but I am certain it was not an old Chinese master!

With this ancient proverbial wisdom, and the not-so-ancient wisdom of an unknown contemporary sage still fresh, we move from proverbs to presumptions. How do these relate to the task before us?

I am presuming that if you are reading this introduction it is because you are contemplating a journey. My presumption is that you are preparing for a spiritual journey and that you have taken at least some of the first steps necessary to prepare for this journey. I also presume, and please excuse me if I am making too many presumptions, that in your preparation for the spiritual journey you have determined that you need a guide. From deep within the recesses of your deepest self, there was something that called you to consider Pierre Teilhard de Chardin as a potential companion. If my presumptions are correct, may I congratulate you on this decision? I think you have made a wise choice, a choice that can be confirmed by yet another source of wisdom, the wisdom that comes from practical experience.

Even an informal poll of experienced travelers will reveal a common opinion; it is very difficult to travel alone. Some might observe that it is even foolish. Still others may be even stronger in their opinion and go so far as to insist that it is necessary to have a guide, especially when you are traveling into uncharted waters and into territory that you have not yet experienced. I am of the personal opinion that a traveling companion is welcome under all circumstances. The thought of traveling alone, to some exciting destination without someone to share the journey with does not capture my imagination or channel my enthusiasm. However, with that being noted, what is simply a matter of preference on the normal journey becomes a matter of necessity when a person embarks on a spiritual journey.

The spiritual journey, which can be the most challenging of all journeys, is experienced best with a guide, a companion, or at the very least, a friend in whom you have placed your trust. This observation is not a preference or an opinion but rather an established spiritual necessity. All of the great saints with whom I am familiar had a spiritual director or a confessor who journeyed with them. Admittedly, at times the saint might well have traveled far beyond the experience of their guide and companion but more often than not they would return to their director and reflect on their experience. Understood in this sense, the director and companion provided a valuable contribution and necessary resource.

When I was learning how to pray (a necessity for anyone who desires to be a full-time and public "religious person"), the community of men that I belong to gave me a great gift.

Between my second and third year in college, I was given a one-year sabbatical, with all expenses paid and all of my personal needs met. This period of time was called novitiate. I was officially designated as a novice, a beginner in the spiritual journey, and I was assigned a "master," a person who was willing to lead me. In addition to the master, I was provided with every imaginable book and any other resource that I could possibly need. Even with all that I was provided, I did not learn how to pray because of the books and the unlimited resources, rather it was the master, the companion who was the key to the experience.

One day, after about three months of reading, of quiet and solitude, and of practicing all of the methods and descriptions of prayer that were available to me, the master called. "Put away the books, forget the method, and just listen." We went into a room, became quiet, and tried to recall the presence of God, and then, the master simply prayed out loud and permitted me to listen to his prayer. As he prayed, he revealed his hopes, his dreams, his struggles, his successes, and most of all, his relationship with God. I discovered as I listened that his prayer was deeply intimate but most of all it was self-revealing. As I learned about him, I was led through his life experience to the place where God dwells. At that moment I was able to understand a little bit about what I was supposed to do if I really wanted to pray.

The dynamic of what happened when the master called, invited me to listen, and then revealed his innermost self to me as he communicated with God in prayer, was important. It wasn't so much that the master was trying to reveal to me what needed to be said; he was not inviting me to pray with the same words that he used, but rather that he was trying to bring me to that place within myself where prayer becomes possible. That place, a place of intimacy and of self-awareness, was a necessary stop on the journey and it was a place that I needed to be led to. I could not have easily discovered it on my own.

The purpose of the volume that you hold in your hand is to lead you, over a period of fifteen days or, maybe more realistically, fifteen prayer periods, to a place where prayer is possible. If you already have a regular experience and practice of prayer, perhaps this volume can help lead you to a deeper place, a more intimate relationship with the Lord.

It is important to note that the purpose of this book is not to lead you to a better relationship with Pierre Teilhard de Chardin, your spiritual companion. Although your companion will invite you to share some of their deepest and most intimate thoughts, your companion is doing so only to bring you to that place where God dwells. After all, the true measurement of a companion for the journey is that they bring you to the place where you need to be, and then they step back, out of the picture. A guide who brings you to the desired destination and then sticks around is a very unwelcome guest!

Many times I have found myself attracted to a particular idea or method for accomplishing a task, only to discover that what seemed to be inviting and helpful possessed too many details. All of my energy went to the mastery of the details and I soon lost my enthusiasm. In each instance, the book that seemed so promising ended up on my bookshelf, gathering dust. I can assure you, it is not our intention that this book end up in your bookcase, filled with promise, but unable to deliver.

There are three simple rules that need to be followed in order to use this book with a measure of satisfaction.

Place: It is important that you choose a place for reading that provides the necessary atmosphere for reflection and that does not allow for too many distractions. Whatever place you choose needs to be comfortable, have the necessary lighting, and, finally, have a sense of "welcoming" about it. You need to be able to look forward to the experience of the journey. Don't travel steerage if you know you will be more comfortable in first class and if the choice is realistic for you. On the other hand, if first class is a distraction and you feel more comfortable and more yourself in steerage, then it is in steerage that you belong.

My favorite place is an overstuffed and comfortable chair in my bedroom. There is a light over my shoulder, and the chair reclines if I feel a need to recline. Once in a while, I get lucky and the sun comes through my window and bathes the entire room in light. I have other options and other places that are available to me but this is the place that I prefer.

Time: Choose a time during the day when you are most alert and when you are most receptive to reflection, meditation, and prayer. The time that you choose is an essential component. If you are a morning person, for example, you should choose a time that is in the morning. If you are more alert in the afternoon, choose an afternoon time slot; and if evening is your preference, then by all means choose the evening. Try to avoid "peak" periods in your daily routine when you know that you might be disturbed. The time that you choose needs to be your time and needs to work for you.

It is also important that you choose how much time you will spend with your companion each day. For some it will be possible to set aside enough time in order to read and reflect on all the material that is offered for a given day. For others, it might not be possible to devote one time to the suggested material for the day, so the prayer period may need to be extended for two, three, or even more sessions. It is not important how long it takes you; it is only important that it works for you and that you remain committed to that which is possible.

For myself I have found that fifteen minutes in the early morning, while I am still in my robe and pajamas and before my morning coffee, and even before I prepare myself for the day, is the best time. No one expects to see me or to interact with me because I have not yet "announced" the fact that I am awake or even on the move. However, once someone hears me in the bathroom, then my window of opportunity is gone. It is therefore important to me that I use the time that I have identified when it is available to me.

Freedom: It may seem strange to suggest that freedom is the third necessary ingredient, but I have discovered that it is most important. By freedom I understand a certain "stance toward life," a "permission to be myself and to be gentle and understanding of who I am." I am constantly amazed at how the human person so easily sets himself or herself up for disappointment and perceived failure. We so easily make judgments about ourselves and our actions and our choices, and very often those judgments are negative, and not at all helpful.

For instance, what does it really matter if I have chosen a place and a time, and I have missed both the place and the time for three days in a row? What does it matter if I have chosen, in that twilight time before I am completely awake and still a little sleepy, to roll over and to sleep for fifteen minutes more? Does it mean that I am not serious about the journey, that I really don't want to pray, that I am just fooling myself when I say that my prayer time is important to me? Perhaps, but I prefer to believe that it simply means that I am tired and I just wanted a little more sleep. It doesn't mean anything more than that. However, if I make it mean more than that, then I can become discouraged, frustrated, and put myself into a state where I might more easily give up. "What's the use? I might as well forget all about it."

The same sense of freedom applies to the reading and the praying of this text. If I do not find the introduction to each day helpful, I don't need to read it. If I find the questions for reflection at the end of the appointed day repetitive, then I should choose to close the book and go my own way. Even if I discover that the reflection offered for the day is not the one that I prefer and that the one for the next day seems more inviting, then by all means, go on to the one for the next day.

That's it! If you apply these simple rules to your journey you should receive the maximum benefit and you will soon find yourself at your destination. But be prepared to be surprised. If you have never been on a spiritual journey you should know that the "travel brochures" and the other descriptions that you might have heard are nothing compared to the real thing. There is so much more than you can imagine.

A final prayer of blessing suggests itself:

> Lord, catch me off guard today.
> Surprise me with some moment of beauty
>   or pain
> So that at least for the moment
> I may be startled into seeing that you are
>   here in all your splendor,
> Always and everywhere,
> Barely hidden,
> Beneath,
> Beyond,
> Within this life I breathe.
>
> *Frederick Buechner*

REV. THOMAS M. SANTA, CSsR
LIGUORI, MISSOURI
FEAST OF THE PRESENTATION, 1999

A Brief Chronology of Pierre Teilhard de Chardin's Life

1881: Pierre Marie Joseph Teilhard de Chardin is born on May 1 at Château de Sarcenat, France; he is the fourth child of a family of minor nobility and the great-nephew of Voltaire. His father collected rocks. Teilhard's interest in geology can be traced to this influence.

1892: Teilhard begins his studies at the Jesuit college in Mongré.

1897: He receives a bachelor's degree in Philosophy and experiences the beginnings of his calling to the religious life.

1898: He receives a bachelor's degree in Mathematics.

1899: He enters the Jesuit noviciate at Aix-en-Provence on March 20. His religious training would take thirteen years.

1901: Teilhard pronounces his first vows. His sister, Louise, dies from meningitis at the age of 12. He begins his long meditations about nature—the first signs of his feelings of connection between the cosmos, nature, and God.

1904: Teilhard leaves for Egypt for advanced studies as well as geological excursions.

1905: Teilhard is appointed professor of physics and chemistry in Cairo; accompanied by his friend, Father Pelletier, he increases his scientific excursions and begins publishing his geological observations.

1911: Teilhard is ordained a priest on August 24 in Hastings, England. His sister, Françoise, a religious in Shanghai, China, dies at the age of 32, due to a smallpox epidemic.

1912: Teilhard begins an apprenticeship at the National Museum of Natural History in Paris, working in the laboratory with the celebrated paleontologist, Marcelin Boule. He begins publishing a series of scientific articles in which synthesis is connected with religion. Aware of the risk to his career, he continues to pursue his work.

1914: World War I begins; he is mobilized as a medic; he refuses all promotions in order to remain close to the men.

1915: Teilhard is a stretcher-bearer, second class, in the Eighth Regiment of the Moroccan artilleries; he writes a great deal in his "Workbooks."

1916: On October 24, his regiment captures Douaumont. Teilhard receives many citations for bravery, including the military medal and the Legion of Honor. Teilhard writes his "War Journals."

1919: In March, he is demobilized; Teilhard is now 39 years old; his two brothers, Gonzague and Olivier, have died in the war. In the summer, he goes to Jersey and writes "The Spiritual Power of Matter" which confuses many people; he receives his certificates in Geology and Botany in Paris.

1920: He receives his certificate in Zoology and prepares his master's thesis at the Catholic Institute, Paris.

1922: On March 22, he successfully defends his doctoral dissertation, "The Mammals of the French Inferior Eocene"; receives a teaching appointment in Geology at the Catholic Institute.

He travels to China—an event that will shape his destiny; meets Father Licent; writes many of his texts for "The Mass on the Altar of the World" in Tien Tsin.

1924: In September, Teilhard returns to France and his teaching position at the Catholic Institute. He writes extensively about the dogma of "original sin" and his new discoveries; his work is sent to Rome and he loses his teaching position; he is greatly upset over his lack of acceptance; he is exiled to China where he will remain for 20 years. He works with the U.S. Geological Service in Peking. He begins to write *The Divine Milieu.* He is recognized as the world authority on the geology of Northern China.

1925 to 1928:
Teilhard takes numerous trips around the Orient, as well as to Somalia and Abyssinia.

1929: Teilhard discovers the first cranium of sinantropos; he returns to Paris to report his findings; he returns to China.

1930 to 1932:
Teilhard takes numerous trips and scientific expeditions into Central Asia; he continues his pursuit of the connection between science and religion and makes the statement: "Nothing is ever destroyed but is elevated, everything that is elevated, converges on Christ."

He visits the U.S., Hawaii, Japan, the Gobi Desert, and London. In 1932, his father, Emmanuel, dies.

1933: Teilhard is upset with the situation in Europe, saying that it is a modern human crisis. He takes trips to Washington D.C., New York, California, Nevada, and the Grand Canyon, then returns to China.

1934 and 1935:
Teilhard is in the midst of research about his discoveries and travels to the Tibetan border; he returns to France briefly and departs for India, the Red Sea, Cashmir, Java, and Bandung. He participates in numerous geological expeditions.

1936: In February, his mother, Berthe-Adèle, dies. In August, his sister, Marguerite, dies.

1937: Teilhard takes numerous trips, one of which is to Philadelphia, where he receives the Mendel medal in recognition of his scientific work. He is very tired and views his personal life as "an endless pilgrimage" but he "takes up the baton and the regimen of separations, which cost me dearly." He writes *The Spiritual Phenomenon.*

1938: He leaves for Peking and writes *Human Energy* during the voyage; other trips to Burma, Java, Vancouver, and New York follow. He travels with Helmut de Terra who makes the comment: "He is exhausted but not a word of criticism or complaint comes out of his mouth...he shares everything with us." In November, he returns to France.

1939: Teilhard writes: "There is something great happening in the world...I am not speaking of politics...everywhere, I find evidence of new beliefs and a spiritual evolution in the world." He gives a series of conferences in Toulouse at the request of his friend, Bruno de Solanges; in June, he leaves to visit the Museum of Natural History in New York; he returns to China where he cofounded, with Father Pierre Leroy, the Geo-biologic Institute of Peking; and he finishes *The Phenomenon of Man.*

1941: Teilhard is now 60 years old; he is feeling the passage of time and is having great difficulty getting his works published.

1943: With Father Leroy, he starts the Geo-biology magazine: *Super Mankind, Super Christ, Super Charity.* He returns to Paris.

1947: He participates in the international conference on paleontology, where he meets and become friends with many notable scientists. On June 1, he has a heart attack. He is called to Rome; he is refused a position at the College of France and his book, *The Phenomenon of Man*, is refused for publication. He reflects: "I am deeply attached to my vow of obedience and would prefer to sacrifice everything than to bring scorn on the integrity of Christ...but there is a deep chasm developing in the intellectual world between the theologians and the scientists...I don't see when my ideas will ever see the light....The Lord will do as he sees fit." He is made an Officer in the Legion of Honor in recognition of his work in geology and paleontology.

1951: Teilhard leaves for his first trip to South Africa in July; he coordinates his research and continues to write. He establishes himself at the Wenner Foundation in New York where he continues his work; he frequently visits the St. Ignatius House where he often celebrates Mass.

1952: He travels to the Southern U.S., and is asked by the foundation to return to South Africa; he returns to New York.

1954: Teilhard returns to France for the last time and visits his birthplace; he returns to New York and states: "My vocation is to devote my life to the discovery of, and in service to, the universal Christ. This is done in complete and absolute faithfulness to the Church, but is decidedly done in the shadow of exile in which I am forced to work....My prayer is to finish my life in prayer as a witness to Jesus."

1954: At a luncheon with friends at the French Consulate, Teilhard states: "I would like to die on the day of Resurrection."

1955: In the first months of the year, Teilhard writes what would be his last book: *The Christic*. On April 10, Easter Sunday in New York, Teilhard says his morning Mass and then attends Mass at St. Patrick's Cathedral; in the afternoon, he attends a concert; he stops to have tea at a friend's home; he experiences sharp pain and faints; he returns to his home and says: "This time, it is terrible." He dies at the age of 74. His funeral is one of great simplicity, held in the chapel of the Jesuit residence, attended by about ten people, including the French Ambassador to the UN and Father Leroy. He is buried in the Jesuit Novitiate Cemetery, some forty miles away, where we can still see his grave, marked by a simple stone with the inscription: "Pierre Teilhard de Chardin, S.J., 1881–1955."

Teilhard's work was published posthumously, of which, his most important work, *The Phenomenon of Man*, was published in 1957.

Introduction

A Great Spiritual Witness

AS WE LEARN MORE about Father Pierre Teilhard de Chardin we cannot doubt that he was an exceptionally rich spiritual witness. As a disciple of Saint Ignatius, faithful always to the practice of holy reflection according to the great tradition of the *Spiritual Exercises*, he had a very intensive interior life which, alone, fortified him to overcome the sufferings he endured. His existence was an astonishing alliance of constant meditation, profound experience of the living God, and the most resolute and advanced involvement in the scientific structures and changes of his time.

Prayer really was the organizing principle of the life of this great Jesuit, and we can only be thankful for his inclusion in this collection. We shall follow his steps and discover that this man of prayer, this person who saw union with God as an echo of the world, is a man who makes a permanent leap into the infinite domain of light and Love without ever being disconnected from the various aspects of his work or from his cultural or intellectual occupations.

To pray with Teilhard is, in many ways, to stand at the crossroads of Revelation and the evolution of the world, the meeting place between the Word of God and the calls and cries of humankind. To pray with Teilhard is to meet a man made of flesh and blood, of intelligence and heart, a scholar and a mystic, one who has suffered but who is still confident. Never, although he was subjected many times to hardship in his family life as well as in his professional life, did he cease to be a witness to hope and to the future. In Teilhard's message, we find a lesson for our time on which we shall meditate fruitfully.

TEILHARD'S MANY-SIDED YET UNIFIED SEARCH

This book will follow Teilhard by means of quotations from a few of his essential texts. This project is made easier by the great spiritual unity of his thinking and his life.

Five great ideas, each comprised of three dimensions, are closely connected: (1) Revelation as seen in God present in the world, the role of Christ, and the meaning of the Cross; (2) Mysticism, as seen in the essential axes, that is, Union, Love, and the progress-detachment relationship; (3) Action, as seen in the importance of work, research, and matter; (4) Presence, as seen in the priest's mission, the deciding sense of the Eucharist, and its cosmic meaning; (5) Hope, as seen in the nature of the Church and the future of Christianity.

From such a great mass of work, I have necessarily chosen texts or prayers that take us through a true spiritual journey. Since my goal was to let Teilhard speak as much as possible for himself, I did not hesitate to give his words priority over my own comments. Given the difficulties that readers encounter when faced with such complex thoughts, I felt it was necessary to highlight Teilhard's own words in order to give you, the reader, a better understanding of the man and also give you a means of accessing the true sources of his spirituality. Thus, we can better follow the steps of the one who was, first and foremost, a great believer and a mystic, before he was an acclaimed scientific thinker.

Abbreviations Used in This Book

THE MOST IMPORTANT SOURCES of Pierre Teilhard de Chardin's writings will be referenced in the following manner:

I, II, III, IV, and so on
The thirteen volumes of de Chardin's work published in French by Éditions du Seuil.

C1, C2, C3
Workbooks, also published by Seuil.

EP *To Be More* (Seuil)

HU *The Hymn of the Universe* (Seuil)

GDP *Making of a Mind* (Grasset)

LDV *Letters From a Traveler*

NLV *New Letters From a Traveler* (Grasset)

LLZ *Letters to Léontine Zanta* (DDB)

HDL *Teilhard de Chardin, the Man and His Meaning* (Mentor-Omega)

BDS *Teilhard de Chardin* by B. De Solanges

ER *Teilhard de Chardin's Thoughts* by E. Rideau

CUE *The Universal Christ and Evolution* by I. Bergeron and A. M. Ernst

15 Days of Prayer With Pierre Teilhard de Chardin

DAY ONE
God's Transparent World

FOCUS POINT

For Teilhard, as well as for so many mystics, God is present in all of Creation, if we would only see. If we would seek God in all things, and see his universal presence surrounding us, we would never hunger, never thirst for him. Instead, we find ourselves so often starving for spiritual food when the banquet of heaven is all around us.

During my life, throughout my entire life, little by little, the world has become ignited, inflamed to my eyes until, all around me, it has become entirely illuminated from within...so much so that when I touched the ground, I experienced the Divine Transparence at the heart of a universe that has become ablaze (XIII, 21). *God, truly only God, excites the mass of the Universe through fermentation by his Spirit* (XII, 171).

This first stage of our journey with Pierre Teilhard de Chardin could only logically begin with a reminder of the importance, to Teilhard, of God's Revelation to the world. If the researcher that Teilhard was, tried, for his entire life, to express the revealed God and the Omega (the culminating point of evolution), the believer that he was saw Tradition in everything, and it was his most intimate conviction that the manifestation of a living and personal God to the world was a certainty. He stated it in the very first lines of his book, *The Divine Milieu*:

> Put yourself here in my place and look: from this privileged vantage point which is not a hard-earned summit reserved to a few chosen people, but which is a solid base built by two thousand years of Christian experience. You are simply going to see the conjunction of two stars whose diverse attractions disorganize your faith. Unadulterated and without confusion, God, the true Christian God, will invade the Universe, right before your eyes. He will penetrate it like a ray of light made of crystal (IV, 26).

Reason, itself, could seriously envisage this Revelation. In fact, Teilhard says: "once accepted, the personality of God, the possibility and even the theoretical probability of a revelation, that is to say, a reflection of God on our conscience, not only does not create difficulties, but is eminently consistent with the nature of things....Among intelligent beings, no presence can remain unknown" (X, 187).

Creation is a great book which is continuously open to human search and contemplation: "No," writes de Chardin, "Creation has never stopped; its action is a great continuous gesture which is spaced across the totality of time." But to perceive God in actions or events, one must first manifest "a faithfulness to follow the ever-rising star of Truth. Only through purity of heart (helped or not by grace, depending on the case) and not pure science, is one able, in a world in a state of movement...to discover with certainty a creator behind the forces of nature" (X, 40).

This God who has involved himself with the world is truly the one which the biblical tradition and Christianity proclaims and reveals to us: the Trinitarian God. Teilhard points out: "If God were not triune, we would not understand that he could...create (and therefore become incarnate) without totally involving himself in the world which he created. From this point of view, the Trinitarian nature of God is not a concept without specific connection to our most real religious needs" (X, 186). On God Incarnate, de Chardin writes: "For God to become incarnate in the World is for him to be born there. However, how is he to be born there if not of an individual?"

Revelation, then, according to Teilhard, becomes Divine Revelation in order to guide both intellect and faith: "Revelation did not come to stop us from searching, but only to tell us how one must seek."

Yet, we are thirsty, thirsty for the Absolute, thirsty to see and know. He says: "If we could see, one could say that all life is there, if not finally, at least essentially." How then, helped by the prophets and mystics, supported by the meaning of the Scriptures, can we not understand that, if we agree to interrupt our foolish pace and our closed thinking, God is transparent to the world?

The world, in all of its dimensions, whether they are the subjects of scientific exploration or contemplation, manifests the presence and actions of God as well as man's own search for meaning. Writes de Chardin: "God made man so that man would find him. God whom we seek to capture through the tentative efforts of our life is the God who surrounds us from everywhere like the world itself. What is missing so that you are able to embrace him? Only one thing, to see him" (IV, 25).

But it is only possible to see God through a just awareness of the totality of the world. Suffering and trials push neither God, nor the idea of God, outside of the world. Teilhard points out: "My entire interior life orients itself and conforms itself more and more to the union to God found in all interior and exterior forces of this world. But for this attitude to be effective, one must exclude nothing from these forces, not death, nor persecution in the realm of ideas. If we believe, everything can be transformed into Our Lord" (LLZ, 73).

That which we call, following Teilhard, "transparency" is nothing more than the illumination of the world, all the way to the darkest of areas, by the universal presence of God: "The great mystery of Christianity is the transparency of God in the Universe...not your Epiphany, Jesus, but your transparency.... The Divine Milieu manifests itself to us like the glow of the interior layers of the being....The Divine Milieu is an atmosphere which is always more brilliant and always more filled with God."

If, for the Christian Tradition, the idea of the Incarnation is essential, it is truly because the "true light, which enlightens everyone, was coming to the world" (Jn 1:9) and, from then on, this world did not resist God. Even better than that, it revealed him. It is God who steers humanity to know him and to love him through events, through the growth or failings of evolution. The modern world suffers from the compartmentalizations which it has established between its fascination for progress and its spiritual search which never stops in its development. Teilhard is surely one of those who had an urgent message to transmit about this point. He wrote: "Lord...you came down into me like a little packet of things and then, suddenly, you unfurled yourself to my eyes, like a universal existence" (XII, 161).

At this point, how could we not concur with this quotation from Ignatius in his *Spiritual Exercises*: "To see how God dwells in creatures, in the elements by the gift of being, in the plants by growth, in animals by feeling, in mankind by the gift of intelligence"?

For Teilhard, all creation is a sign and the Word of God, even in the most abrupt or most violent aspects of its appearance. Faced with its complexity, our responsibility only grows: "Nature is a force with two faces: on one hand, a burden and threat to our lives and, on the other hand, it brings physical happiness and the joy of growth. Thus, the spiritual force of matter is and will be captured for God."

Humanity is obligated, by reason of its very nature, to return to the source. Teilhard explains: "Precisely because he is infinitely profound and unique, God is infinitely close and spread out everywhere. But our God pushes the limits of the differentiation of his creatures; he concentrates it in them to the extreme."

For Teilhard, the "transparency" of the world is definitely realized through evolution's constant movement, like a brilliance that stretches to invade everywhere in a continuous creation: "Faith," he says, "is the practical conviction that the Universe, in the hands of the Creator, continues to be the clay which he molds to his liking in numerous possibilities. There are no rigid determinants of matter...but the supple combinations of the Holy Spirit which give consistency to the universe."

Yes, truly, "the world is full, it is full of the Absolute." Should we not adhere to God through all the extensions of the universe? Without restraining the essential role of faith in the discovery and recognition of God throughout the appearances of the world, Teilhard says:

> If we believe, everything is illuminated and takes shape around us, risk no longer exists, and success takes on an incorruptible fullness; pain becomes a visit and a caress from God. If we hesitate, the rock remains dry, the sky black, the waters treacherous and swift. And we can hear the voice of our Master in the midst of our spoiled life: "O ye of little faith, why have you doubted me?" (EP, 88).

The world, through faith in a living God, becomes that altar on which, as much by the forces which make the world grow as by those which make it die, is realized the most luminous act of union and the most powerful exchange of love. Teilhard explains:

> The person who would passionately love Jesus, who is hidden in the forces which make the earth grow, for that person the earth will maternally lift him up in a giant embrace and make him contemplate the face of God....The person who would have passionately loved Jesus hidden in the forces which would make the earth die, for that person the crumbling earth will maternally enclose him in a giant embrace, and with the earth, he will awaken in the embrace of God (XIII, 151).

REFLECTION QUESTIONS

Do I seek God in all things? Can I look at someone I do not care for, and see the presence of God dwelling within that person? Can I see with eyes of faith, and love with a heart that trusts in the goodness of all God's Creation?

BIBLE READING

The suggested Bible passage for meditation is Acts 16:16–34.

PRAYER

God our Father, give us the gift to perceive your luminous presence in the world and throughout history. Amen.

DAY TWO

The Universal Christ and the Divine Milieu

FOCUS POINT

By our free will and by the grace of God we can choose to take an active part in the Church, the Body of Christ. We can open our eyes and recognize that we have been transformed by Christ—reunited with the Divine, at peace with all Creation.

Glorious Christ, you are the influence secretly infused into the midst of all matter. You are the blinding Center where the innumerable fibers of the multiple join together. You are inexorably powerful like the world and warm like life. Your forehead is made of snow, eyes of fire, your feet are more sparkling than infused gold. Your hands imprison the stars. You who are the first and the last, you are the living, the dead, and the arisen....It is you who my being called with a desire as vast as the universe: You are truly my Lord and my God (XIII, 34).

Christ is at the very center of Teilhard's reasoning. He is the beating heart of his existence. In the face of this example, we are driven to ask ourselves: what faith do I have in a living and present Christ? Am I able to make the teachings of this wise Jesuit an inspiration for my own benefit? Along with Teilhard, can I say: "With a renewal of resolution and of enlightenment, I dedicate my life and myself in individual service to the body of Christ, to be felt, loved, and promoted, in all the places where the Spirit is born and manifests itself for God in the midst of the universe and for human effort" (C, 4)?

To believe in Jesus is not merely a simple juxtaposition of religious convictions but a free action—one that culminates in a personal relationship of love. The universal and cosmic dimension that Teilhard recognized in the risen Christ does not dissolve into a vague syncretism but is expressed in accord with all historical and mystical facts of the Christian Tradition.

Maintains de Chardin: "Christ is not a superfluous accessory added to the world, a king like we have made of him, an owner....He is the alpha and the omega, the principle and the goal, the stone foundation and the key to the vault, the Plenitude and the Fulfiller. He is the one who consumes, the one who gives everything its consistency. Toward him and through him, all life and inner light of the world becomes, through turmoil and effort, the universal convergence of all created spirit. Christ is the unique center, precious and constant, who sparkles at the summit yet-to-come into the world, opposing the obscure regions, which are eternally declining, where our knowledge ventures when it follows the pathway of matter and the past" (IX, 60).

At this point, it might be well to meditate on Saint Paul's affirmations in his letter to the Colossians (1:15–20). Teilhard recognizes himself in these and other expressions of recapitulation and unification (Ephesians 4:9ff.; 1 Corinthians 15:23ff.; John 1; and John 12:32). But this affirmation of Christ as the center cannot be isolated from a comprehension of the global dynamics of Revelation. Christ is the manifestation of God the Creator and becomes, through the Resurrection, the one who fulfills and sums up everything in him.

According to Teilhard, the historic and human dimension of the Incarnation is fundamental: "If omitted, the historical reality of Christ, the divine omnipresence which impassions us, becomes like all other dreams of the metaphysical: uncertain, vague, conventional, without decisive experimental control to impose itself on our spirits, without moral direction to assimilate itself into our lives" (IV, 140).

The reference to the Gospel and to its human and cultural outlines, to its vivid language and to its social and religious rootedness, are essential in order to understand the universal implication of salvation. For Teilhard, Christ was born to Mary and died on the Cross: "No matter how far we allow ourselves to be carried into the divine spaces of mystical Christianity, we can not escape Jesus as he is in the Gospel."

The connection is firmly maintained between the Incarnation and the final accomplishment: "Truly," writes de Chardin, "the more we reflect upon the profound laws of evolution, the more we convince ourselves that the universal Christ would not know to appear at the end of time, at the summit of the world, if he had not previously been established there along the route, by the pathway of his birth." Only this face of Christ could satisfy the ambition of our time. Neither a God of limited scope, nor a religion with limited and petty outlines, will ever satisfy a person who is thirsty for the absolute: "Could Christ diminish God....Oh, how this mortal suspicion fades so easily...right from the very instant when, sensitive to modern mysticism, we perceive...that a God, historically incarnate, is the only one who could satisfy, not only the inflexible rules of the universe, where nothing happens or appears except by the pathway of birth, but the irrepressible aspirations of our Spirit" (XIII, 66).

Teilhard calls Christ, when measured against the immensity of the world and in accordance with the great writings of Saint Paul, the Universal Christ. He is none other than the risen Christ who is spreading his power all the way to the limits of the universe: "The Universal Christ, as I understand it, is a synthesis of Christ and the Universe." In fact, the expressions "Cosmic Christ," "Christic," and "Divine Milieu," like that of "Universal Christ," arise as new words that seek to express the same reality. As big as the universe reveals itself to be, it could not escape the transforming and enlightening action of Christ. Says de Chardin: "The universe is impregnated, right to its material core, with the influence of the superhuman nature of Christ. The presence of the Incarnate Word penetrates everything like a universal element."

As the Incarnation of God, Christ could be no less than God in his infinite force. Faced with physical and spiritual immensities, the power of growth, and forces of engulfment, only the Christ of glory is able to "encompass the formidable dimensions of the universe."

But how do we understand the Resurrection? For Teilhard, in addition to the action of Christ and his work of salvation, the Resurrection has a decisive significance for the evolution of the universe: "We seek too much to see the Resurrection as an apologetic and temporary event, like Christ's short sojourn in the tomb. The Resurrection is something altogether different and much more than that. It is a 'formidable' cosmic event. It signifies the actual taking of possession, by Christ, of his functions as the universal Center....When we are faced with a universe whose spiritual and physical immensity reveals itself to us as more and more vertiginous, and when we are frazzled by the ever-growing weight of energy and glory that must be placed upon the son of Mary so that we may have the right to continue to adore him, let us think of the Resurrection" (IX, 92).

Today and always, the risen Christ is present to the world; he reveals God to us. The divine milieu has a center. In him, all the elements of the universe are connected in their greater interiority. The one who unites the elements and the people by incorporating them into his body is Christ. As de Chardin prays: "I love you, Jesus, you are the source, the active and life-giving milieu."

To be united to Christ is to leave what is often only surface desolation. Teilhard says: "Let us leave the surface. And without leaving the world, let us enter into God. There and from there, in him and through him, we will have it all and have charge of it all. All of the flowers and lights we have had to abandon in order to be faithful to life, there, one day, we will retrieve their essence and their spark. The beings we despair over attaining and influencing, they are there, all reunited by the point which is the most vulnerable, the most receptive, and the most enriching to their substance...and, at the same time, we will sense that, at our very depths, the fullness of our forces of action and adoration come together effortlessly" (IV, 138).

Later, we will delve into another way, into the consequences of this union with Christ; but here it is good for us, with an attitude of prayer, to understand that hope, which the world needs desperately, does not presuppose a flight from earthly realities or a suspicion of the visible or the tangible. To the contrary, hope integrates, into their full dimensions, all of the aspects of history and existence. That is so because Jesus, the eternal Word and the man from Nazareth, was raised from the dead.

Prays Teilhard: "Lord, because in my instincts and in the opportunities of my life I have never stopped seeking you and placing you at the center of all universal matter, it is in the resplendence of a universal transparency that I will have the joy to close my eyes....Jesus, as a 'little child' in the arms of his Mother—conforming to the great law of birth—you have entered my childlike soul. And this is what repeats and prolongs the circle of your growth in me through the Church....Your humanity as a Palestinian has, little by little, spread everywhere, like a never-ending rainbow where your presence, without destroying anything, but by superanimating it, penetrates any other presence around me" (XIII, 67).

REFLECTION QUESTIONS

Do I recognize Jesus Christ as the center of the universe? Do I recognize Jesus Christ as the center of my life? Do I feel the transforming power his Resurrection has brought to my life and to my relationship with God?

BIBLE READING

The suggested Bible passage for meditation is Colossians 1:11–23.

PRAYER

Risen Christ, you are at the heart of our existence and the One who frees and fulfills. Amen.

DAY THREE

The Meaning of the Cross

FOCUS POINT

That God would sacrifice his earthly life on the Cross, for *our* sake—His suffering shows us the greatest love of all. Through our own suffering we can unite ourselves with God, and model his great love for our fellow brothers and sisters. We can know and share in God's love through suffering.

It is perfectly true that the Cross signifies an escape from a sensory world and, even in a sense, a rupture with this world. By the terms of the Ascension, we are invited, in fact, we are forced, to jump over a threshold, a critical point, where we lose our footing within the zone of sensory reality. This final excess, foreseen and accepted right from the first step, inevitably throws a light, a particular spirit, on all our actions. And that is precisely where Christian folly lies in the eyes of the sages who don't want to risk a single good which they actually possess on a total "beyond." ... We will lift ourselves to the sum-

mits which appear foggy to our human eyes and where the crucifix invites us by a path which is the road of universal progress. The royal road of the Cross is truly the road of human effort, supernaturally rectified and prolonged. In order to have fully heard the meaning of the Cross, we no longer run the risk of finding life to be sad or ugly. We have only become more attentive to its incomprehensible seriousness (IV, 138).

Teilhard's writings about the Cross lead us to recognize two particular aspects that highlight the originality of his thinking.

The first aspect concerns spiritual theology: the perspective that Teilhard almost exclusively insists upon—without denying all other aspects. This aspect regards a connection or tension, a dynamic of fulfillment achieved through violent rupture and suffering. Christ was truly the one who was nailed to the Cross, who died through an overabundance of Love, signifying the crucified world. Through his unique action, he died to save humanity, which was locked in sin. But this Christ was God. And God, by the Cross, according to another set of logic, became the culmination of Revelation. The light was not absent in Golgotha, it was another light: "At first glance this bloody body could appear funereal to us. Does it not radiate out of the night?" The light shines forth from God's night, the one of creation and birth—the one of upheaval and of confidence. Teilhard explains: "For the Christian, it is not a question of disappearing into the shadows, but of arising into the light of the Cross."

The second aspect of Teilhard's theology of the Cross concerns a personal experience which could help us understand his writings. From the beginning to the end of his life, this man lived the painful alliance between research and rupture, certainty and hesitation, faithfulness and condemnation. He said, in reference to it: "Each and every spiritual adventure is a Calvary" and "I didn't think that someone could suffer so much." For him, the tearing apart had become almost habitual: family, friends, institutions, all of this never without the inner project being interrupted or fundamentally challenged. The Cross had been truly experienced like a threshold of emergence and a victory, with Christ, over the forces of resignation or capitulation.

To Teilhard, the Cross was an integral part of the Christian message and of the faith of the Church. Since he did not want to make a theological study out of this particular point, he did not develop the connecting elements which could only be inferred, including the connection between the Cross and redemption through Christ. Indisputably, here, spiritual logic swings to the side of the Incarnation and—this point is not without interest—places the Cross as an element of the world with the ability to manifest something other than terror, dislocation, or total death. Says de Chardin: "Too often, the Cross has been presented for our adoration—less as a sublime goal that we would attain by surpassing ourselves than as a symbol of sadness, restriction, and repulsion" (IV, 115).

For Teilhard and his spirituality, the Incarnation, Passion, and Resurrection are closely connected. The Cross is the clearest sign of the paradox of progress and detachment which we grapple with in the sixth stage. "It [the Cross] is erected at the head of the route which leads to the highest summit of creation. There exist dual unique movements which correspond to each other in order to preserve it from the provocations of matter: immersion and emergence, participation with things and sublimation, possession and renunciation, passage and being led."

Is the Incarnation exempt from these movements? No. For the believer, the Cross is a sign of both extreme proximity and of extreme abandon. Love reaches its highest at the point where suffering dominates. Within the ultimate act of salvation, which is an act of love and not subterfuge, detachment is etched. For Christ, his self-abandonment to the Father was the opening to the total light and to life. For Teilhard, action implies detachment: "In fact, such is the living logic of the action, that we could not conquer ourselves and grow unless we die, little by little, to ourselves. To act with dignity, usefully…is to unite ourselves. But to unite oneself is to transform oneself with something greater than our self."

The Cross symbolizes metamorphosis and transfiguration, childbirth and light. In Saint John's Gospel, the hour of the Cross is at the same moment the hour of glory: "Now my soul is troubled. And what should I say—'Father, save me from this hour'? No, it is for this reason that I have come to this hour. Father, glorify your name" (Jn 12:27–28).

The Cross symbolizes tension and interiorization. Writes de Chardin: "When, through ecstacy or through death, God definitively wants to submit and unite himself with the Christian, we could say that he carries it out only by tightening the bond through love and through obedience in the extension of his effort."

For Teilhard, the Cross must not, in any case, disappear from the horizon of faith nor be diminished in its consequences in the midst of evangelization of the new covenant. Very much to the contrary, what we must avoid is for the Cross to be misunderstood or not understood at all, or for it to become an obstacle in the proclamation of the living God, even if the Cross remains forevermore a scandal and a question. One must avoid misunderstanding without, however, stopping the inevitable rupture.

The strongest expression of Teilhard's themes regarding the Cross is found in his article from 1952 entitled "What the World Awaits From the Church of God at This Moment: A Generalization and a Deepening of the Meaning of the Cross" (X, 257). At this point, let us note just how important the unity that exists between the conception and expression of the message is to Teilhard. The Cross then integrates itself into the whole where the principal signs of salvation, by reason of their differences, are complementary in meaning with regard to the Christian Tradition. As de Chardin explains: "A baptism or purification becomes a subordinated element within the total divine gesture of lifting up the world. A Cross represents much more than expiated sin; it symbolizes the ascent of Creation beyond the effort. Blood circulates and gives life even more if it is not shed. The Lamb of God is carrying, along with sins, the weight of the progress of the world. The idea of forgiveness and sacrifice sheds itself through its self-enrichment, through the idea of consummation and conquering. The redemptive Christ, in other words, fulfills himself without diminishing his suffering face, through the dynamic bounty of an evolutionary Christ."

The Cross truly occupies the central place, dominating the Eucharist and accompanying all prayer and Christian sacraments, as the sign of recognition. If it remains as such, that which cannot be contested without disfiguring Christianity, then what is it that must be changed?

Teilhard states further: "In order to reign over an earth which has been suddenly awakened and made conscious of a biological movement which leads us toward the front, the Cross (under the threat of being incompatible with human nature which it has claimed to save) must, at all costs and at once, manifest itself to us as a sign, not only of evasion, but of progression. It must shine in our eyes, not only as a means of purification but like a 'driving force.' But is such a transformation 'without deformation' possible? Yes, I would answer, it is possible and even required, if we go to the heart of things, because there is nothing more traditional in the Christian spirit."

Let us take note that Teilhard does not exclude, but include. He says: "Not only, but even more...." His proposal is not to separate the redemptive action from the eschatological (theological concern with death and final destiny) dimension of the world in the making. Atonement, yes, but atonement and evolution. The Cross destroys the logic of the strong and the proud but it must not be a barrier between the Word of God and man's search.

He continues: "In summary, in spite of the profound modifications happening in our phenomenal vision of the World, the Cross is always standing upright. It stands up even straighter at the crossroads of all values and problems, at the very heart of humanity. It can and must continue, more than ever, to be the place where the division takes place between those who climb and those who descend" (X, 260).

REFLECTION QUESTIONS

How do I view the Cross? Do I see it as a goal for which I strive, as a sad reminder, or as something to avoid? Do I seek to unite myself with the Cross? Do I seek to accept the suffering and transformation that accompanies the Cross? Can I understand the Cross as a means of uniting myself to Christ in suffering?

BIBLE READING

The suggested Bible reading for meditation is John 12:1–36.

PRAYER

Spirit of God on the Cross, give us the confidence to hold vigil in the night of our faith. Amen.

DAY FOUR
A Mystic of Union

FOCUS POINT

Teilhard de Chardin was an apostle of the unity of all Creation. He was also a lived example of the effort to unite what seems to be contradictory experience—intellect and adoration, science and religion, soul and body, evolution and creation. How do I attempt to unify the competing questions of my life—the struggle between work and prayer, pragmatism and love, worldly achievement and supernatural happiness?

It's not a confidential conversation nor a hand-to-hand battle that we need, but a heart-to-heart communication. Under these current conditions, the more I scrutinize the fundamental question about the future of the earth, the more I perceive that the generating principle of its unification is not to be found or finally to be sought in the individual contemplation of the truth nor in the individual desire suggested by Something, but is found through the common attraction exerted by the same Someone (V, 99).

The principle of unity which saves sinful creation which is on its return to dust is Christ. By the force of his attraction, by the light of his life, by the cement of his very being, Jesus came to re-establish, in the world, the harmony of efforts and the conversion of persons (XII, 143).

The dominant characteristic of Teilhard's personality— the one which, in all cases, singles him out and allows him to seriously envision the timelessness of his work—is not connected to either science or philosophy, which he greatly honored through his research and writings, but is connected to Teilhard's spiritual life. He was a mystic, a prayerful person, and a visionary. Faithful to the great Ignatian tradition of prayer and meditation, he never stopped feeding his thirst for the absolute and for his unifying vision. His friend and collaborator, Pierre Leroy, called this characteristic "intelligent piety." Bruno de Solages spoke of Teilhard's "mystical spirituality." Father Noir, just at the time of publication of de Chardin's *Retreat Workbooks*, about which we hear a great deal, wrote: "Ignatius' passion for an ever greater glory of God is translated to Teilhard by his adoration and proclamation of a Christ who is always greater, who is the only one who is able to fill the higher state of an evolution in progress towards its plenitude."

Adoration, when speaking of all of Revelation, drove Teilhard to a ever stronger need to seek unity in the dual experience, exterior and interior, that he had of reality. Teilhard's mysticism was there from the beginning and fundamentally indicated by the double dimension: cosmic and Christic. The double passion of the world and of God characterized his entire life, right from his childhood.

The human experience is a demanding search to contact the essential unity of the universe, to locate a foreshadowed but mysterious source. In 1917, Teilhard wrote: "The soul carries within itself the requirement of a single essential element and the assurance that this essential element exists for it....The fundamental mystical state is an energetic feeling of omnipresence, an apprehension of the perception of something which is universal, constant, absolute, the love of all, centered around One."

For Teilhard, this state does not, furthermore, come from a pre-scientific conception of the world. He would speak of a modern mysticism: "By modern mysticism I mean the need, the science, and the art of reaching, at the same time and each through the other, both the universal and the spiritual, and achieving a freedom from all multiplicity or spiritual weight. That is it, more profound than all ambition for pleasure, riches, and power, the essential dream of the human soul."

But this state, in radical fashion, keeps itself distant, by its own definition, from dangerous naturalistic mysticisms by giving a childlike slant or a hint of illumination to the best beginnings. This state is an adhesion to the personal God of the Revelation through whom the meaning of the world and history is progressively revealed. The unity of exterior and interior reality can only come about through the experience of the presence of God to the universe and to humanity. Teilhard says: "By taking hold of the earth, I can adhere to You....From the milieu of his dream, the mystic is a great realist" (XII, 182).

Beginning from this statement, Teilhard unfurls an authentic and complete spirituality by going beyond the theoretical or doctrinal aspect of his work which is expressed by the reference to an interior experience where Christ is the center. It is an experience which does not scatter humanity but which, to the contrary, gives it its full meaning. In his first war journals, this point of view is already made clear. He writes of his goals: "To be an integral Christian, but remaining more human than anyone else....To make sure that the Universal Christ does not become a knot for my own speculations but arises from the real depth of my practical experience." *The Divine Milieu* is the result and the decisive representation of this early conviction: "The Kingdom of God is within ourselves. When Christ will appear...in the midst of humanity, he will make manifest a metamorphosis which is slowly fulfilled under his influence. Therefore, in order to hasten his coming, let us work to better understand the process according to which the Holy Presence is created and develops within us" (IV, 158).

Teilhard's spirituality is thus defined by a close bond to Christ who is the revealer of God and source of the true transformation of the world. As he avers: "I would give my life so that finally the God from On High and from Before is discovered, that is to say, the Universal Christ, outside of whom we risk suffocation." In regard to this, let us remember the importance the Jesuit Teilhard attaches to faithfulness, right to the end, to annual retreats, and how conscious he was of his ministry as a priest, with the responsibility to reveal to people, in one and the same witness, both the grandeur of the world and God's beauty.

In the evolution of the universe there exists a logic of unity. Perceived in the complex mechanisms of the different phases of the world's organization, this unity is culminated in the act of adoration and the requirements of love. The creation is characterized by a process of successive unifications with the goal of a perfect union at the end. Teilhard, wanting to account for the constant presence of God in the created world while maintaining the principle of the evolution of the world, used the expression, certainly a delicate one, of "creative union," of which the difficulty for philosophical understanding was equaled only by his spiritual ambition: to better account for the fact that God the Creator did not separate himself from the act of creation.

God created by uniting, thus making the role of Christ unique. Through Christ's humanity, the union of the presence of God and the expansion of this presence throughout evolution were accomplished. In his glorious Resurrection, he was "the summit of the cone," in which everything is summarized: "The philosophy of the creative union...is only the development, generalization, and extension to the universe of what the Church teaches us about the growth of Christ. It is the philosophy of the universe, conceived in relation to the notion of the mystical body. I have discovered this above all: seeking to love and find Christ everywhere is the only way this principle of unity can be understood" (XII, 222).

Teilhard's mysticism of union led him to see the developing world in an overall vision. He was a man of synthesis and coherence whose source was none other than God. Only he could allow the whole to "be held by the top." The principle of the union of all elements which make up the process of evolution is only reached through a similar attitude of observation and interiorization. Science and mysticism, then, are understood as being like the two eyes of the same glance looking towards the absolute.

Teilhard connects the possibility of synthesis to the glorious energy of the risen Christ. It is an energy which permits the progressive realization of the body. Coherence, in no way, could be a stroke of luck or the fruit of only human enterprise. One must start from de Chardin's principle of one God and not from the human capacity as affected by the multiplicity. Teilhard starts from the top and not from the bottom: "If I take the universe by going up from less to more, I would have continuous 'obstacles' which would prevent me from advancing. The inferior supports but does not completely determine the superior. I will only obtain a synthesis by descending from the superior, that is to say, from the body of Christ."

But the synthesis is only, in experimental terms, the fruit of the invisible reality. Everything comes from the One who faces the dispersion of the world through the creative force of his love, which is a thousand times more unifying than sin is divisive. The Christian message must be one of love and unity, progress and communion.

Teilhard continues: "Through the persistent effort of Christian thinking, the anguishing enormity of the world converges, little by little, toward the top until it transforms itself into a hearth of loving energy....Let us join the body to the head, the base to the summit: and abruptly, there will be a plenitude which spurts forth" (XI, 139).

This plenitude, of which prayer makes us fully conscious, contributes to human happiness. It pushes human beings ahead, in an opposite direction from all the temptations to regress, divide, or despair. It gives access to eternity.

REFLECTION QUESTIONS

Teilhard proclaims a Christ who is at the very center of all experience and progress. Do I see Christ moving ever closer to the center of my own being? Teilhard promises a Christ whose Divine Presence dwells within us. How do I nurture the growth of this Divine Presence? Teilhard connects an abundance of energy to the glorious power of the risen Christ. Do I rely on this strength to travel along my own path to union with God?

BIBLE READING

The suggested Bible passage for meditation for this day is John 15:1–7.

PRAYER

Trinitarian God, keep us in communion with your truth and protect us from all divisions. Amen.

DAY FIVE

The Strength of Love

FOCUS POINT

For Teilhard, Christian love is love of God, love of neighbor, and love of all creation. It is a universal power that charges the universe and evolves it toward the Divine Center. This love given to us by God is tremendously dynamic. Have you opened your life to the transforming power of God's love?

"Love one another by recognizing that at the heart of each person, the same God resides." These words, said some two thousand years ago, today, tend to reveal themselves as the essential structural basis of what we call progress and evolution. These words are part of the scientific domain of necessary cosmic energies and laws.

To love God and our neighbor is then not just simply an act of veneration or benevolence which is superimposed upon our other individual preoccupations. It is life itself, life within expressed in the integrity of its aspirations, battles, and ac-

complishments, and embraced in a spirit of closeness and unification with everything else that matters to the Christian, if indeed he wants to be a Christian (V, 100).

In Teilhard's spirituality, love holds an important place because it is the fundamental energy, the manifestation of God in Creation. It guides the evolution of the world by etching the constant call for union and fulfillment into the depths of people and their actions.

The mysticism of union only finds its reason for existence in love and through love. The paradox is that Teilhard, at no time, ever theologically developed this theme, nor did he make it the subject of a specific study. He gave reference to it, however, at key places: in his first book, *The Phenomenon of Man* (I, 293); in an essential part of *The Divine Milieu* (IV, 181); and in *Human Energy* (VI, 180).

Teilhard wrote the following two phrases as a motif for *The Divine Milieu*: "*Sic Deus dilexit mundum*" (God so loved the world) referring to John 3:16; and "For those who love the world." He repeated again the end of Saint Ignatius' *Spiritual Exercises*, "*Ad Amorem*," meaning that "love must be put more into actions than into words....Love consists of mutual communication between the lover and the loved."

It is certain that the experience of the union between humans and God depends as much on the person's participation with the creation of the world as it does on his capacity to love. How can we avoid an overvaluation of the actions and the risk of an idolatry of the effort if not by being conscious of love and all its components? Teilhard reminds us: "Love is the most universal, most tremendous, and most mysterious of the cosmic energies....Socially, we pretend to ignore it in science, in business, and in meetings when, surreptitiously, it is everywhere" (VI, 40).

For him, love is so much more than a unifying principle that permits a precise integration, at the same time, of progress and rupture, life and death. Love is the central reality, a total manifestation of God, and the organizing force of the world. Teilhard places love as the principle of all true synthetic knowledge because it is exactly the principle of the genesis of the universe. He writes: "Love has always been carefully separated from the realistic and positive constructions of the world. We must, one day, decide to recognize, in him, the fundamental energy of life, or, if you prefer, the only natural milieu in which the ascending movement of evolution could be prolonged" (V, 75).

But this love is not an anonymous force. It comes from God. In *The Phenomenon of Man*, love, which is the general property of all life, is the actual and constant manifestation of the Omega on the world. Love is a personal reality. It is Christ, the hearth of unification for the world by an eternal action of communion and of sublimation. All of the values which are progressively expressed during the evolution of humanity will be derived from this first and ultimate reality.

In *Human Energy*, Teilhard developed this conviction even more deeply. Love is the "totalizer" principle of human energy. Through love, a totalization of individual acts is accomplished, acts of individuals upon themselves and of individuals in humanity. This totalization is produced by Christ, the total revelation of God, the Alpha and the Omega. Teilhard writes: "Whether he lives or dies, by his life and by his death, in some way, the Christian consumes his God at the same time as he is dominated by him....Christ's essential message holds true in the proclamation of a 'Divine Paternity.' ...Many times, human religious gropings have already approached the idea that the God-Spirit could only be attained through the Spirit. But it is only through Christianity that the movement could reach its definitive expression and consistency....God-Love will only finally be attained through love. That is the psychological revolution and the secret of Christian progress" (VI, 193).

The theme of eternal unifying love appeared strongly as a background, beginning with his first war-time writings, particularly in *The Eternal Feminine*, which was a symbolic transposition of the biblical book the Song of Solomon. Here de Chardin writes: "I appeared at the time of the beginning of the world. From even before time, I came from the hands of God....Everything in the universe is made through union and fertility, by gathering the elements that are seeking each other, two by two, joining them together, and they are reborn through a third thing...I am the essential woman" (XII, 281). In this work, the "eternal feminine" refers not only to women, but to Mary and the Church.

The man-woman connection is essential for evolution and represents the strongest expression of love; in reality, it represents the universe advancing "toward man and through the woman." As de Chardin says: "The whole question is that they recognize one another....If man perceives the universal reality which shines through the flesh, he will then discover what was perverting and deceiving his power to love....Through love, the attraction to the Center, toward which everything converges, is etched and felt" (VI, 41).

Teilhard, in many of his homilies for marriage ceremonies, referred to the connection between the presence of God and the vital significance of the union, in love, of the man and the woman. Let us cite a few lines of the most significant text: "If both of you want to respond to the call [to grace] that a life, enriched by God, makes for you today...believe in this intangible support.

Believe in the support of the Spirit, as it has in a long list of past unions which are the same as your own….Remember that you carry the responsibility before God and the universe within you.

Believe in the Spirit before you. Creation never ends….May your union never be a closed embrace, but come to fulfillment through action…through effort toward the same goal, always greater, and always passionately loved.

Believe, then, in the Spirit between you….It is through a constant exchange of thoughts, affection, dreams, and prayers that you will, above all, come to know each other. Only through that will you know that there exists no satiety, deception, and no limits through the Spirit beyond the flesh. Only there, will your love have freedom, which is the greatest issue" (XIII, 159).

Love holds the universe together, assuring equilibrium for each living being as well as the interior growth and mystical conscience of believers. In this sense, love is necessary and becomes the source of inevitable requirements. Comments de Chardin: "It is impossible to love Christ without loving others…and impossible to love others without getting closer to Christ through this same action. This inevitable union has always taken place in the interior life of the saints by means of an overabundance of love for all those people who carry within themselves the seed of eternal life."

Many of Teilhard's texts insist on the need for love of others, through the logic of the union with God: "My God, I admit that for a long time I have been and still am, alas, unwilling to love my neighbor….My God, make it so that I reflect your face to the lives of others….Jesus, Savior of human activity, to whom you bring a reason to act, Savior of human suffering to whom you bring a value to life, be the salvation of human unity by forcing us to abandon our smallness and, with your support, to venture out onto the unknown ocean of charity" (IV, 184).

Teilhard's mysticism is completely distinguished by a faithfulness to the inner call of love which is nothing other than the mysterious and unutterable footprint of God. He was the first to live what he wrote in *The Spiritual Phenomenon* (VI, 115), for the "motivation from without." He writes: "In truth, each of us is called to respond to a universal note with a pure and unutterable harmony. As God's love progresses in our hearts, we will sense the exuberant simplicity of a thrust where the nuance of passion and action will combine themselves and we will come closer to the full expression of our personality."

REFLECTION QUESTIONS

Do I see all people as loved by God, or do I make subtle yet exclusionary distinctions? Do I act as if love is what matters most to me as a Christian, or do I actually value material things more? Prayer is the language of our love for God. Do I spend adequate time and energy in the mutual communication of prayer? Do I pretend to love Christ yet fail to demonstrate my love through action? Do I see love for Christ, not as a passive experience but as passionate action and utter faithfulness?

BIBLE READING

The suggested Bible passage for meditation is 1 Corinthians 13.

PRAYER

Lord Jesus, may your message and example of love become the horizon for the Church and for our lives. Amen.

DAY SIX

Progress and Detachment

FOCUS POINT

In the scope of Teilhard de Chardin's thinking, our human effort is a loving collaboration with God. At the same time that we strive toward progress and growth, we face unexpected events that weigh down our lives in anguish. It is essential to our humanity that we are at the same time powerful and powerless, attached and detached, passionate yet indifferent.

I found myself thinking again about a subject which, for me, has always been a problem with my interior life...the reconciliation of progress and detachment, of impassioned legitimate love for the entire world and the single search for the Kingdom of heaven, that is, the dilemma of how to be as Christian as anyone else while being more human than any (HDL, 348).

The more I live my life, the more I come to know that true rest is comprised of "renouncing myself" to my sense of self, that is to say, in resolutely admitting that it is of no importance to be either happy or unhappy (in the current sense of the words). Success or personal satisfaction does not warrant that we stop there if we have it, or that we be troubled if it escapes us or if it's late in coming. The only thing that is of value is faithful actions for the world in God (LDV, 126).

Spiritual life is the constant dialectic and combination of development and interiority, of the without and the within. Here, I am thinking of the astonishing connection that Paul made between strength and weakness (2 Cor 12:9–10) or between Christ's glory and humility (Phil 2:6–11). Teilhard, a person who was passionate about both research and the future, wanted to be both faithful to the gospel and vigilant of the tradition of Ignatius. For Teilhard, that interior battle was very productive.

In fact, having mentioned the mysticism of union and the strength of love, it is difficult to omit the place that renunciation and suffering held in Teilhard's life, an aspect about which little is known and much is misunderstood in spite of his many writings. Teilhard held an attitude of "indifference," in the Ignatian sense of the term. In this sense, the Christian is, at the same time, both the most "attached and the most detached of humans." Teilhard says: "The creation or organization of material energy removes the comfort zone where egoism and attachments lie. Little by little, the worker of the soil is no longer his own master....Human effort is a loving, shaky collaboration which we give into divine hands. It is both personal fulfillment and embellishment but also a gift that has just begun. It is an attachment to Creation but it is also a complete detachment. Something dominates: an impetus towards heaven, a laborious and painful ecstacy through matter, personal progress, and a renunciation in God."

At the core of these convictions, de Chardin's "mystical" experience of World War I, a kind of crucible of suffering and contemplation where, at the same time, total deprivation and prayer, trial and confidence, and an apprehension of "everything" through "nothingness" took place.

This phase of his life had a profound impact on him, progressively leading him to a total transformation of his entire being into "a live wire, sparking his scientific and anthropological research until his death."

Teilhard's thoughts about this plan were best synthesized in his book, *The Divine Milieu: An Essay on the Interior Life*. Man is, all at once and at the same time, acting and dominated. The hidden part of the iceberg, by far the most important, determines our existence. The secret phase of a meeting with the angel could either conclude with confident self-abandonment to God, a rebellion, or the tragic discovery of powerlessness. These hidden and mysterious forces which cross and influence the night ocean of our personality are called the "passivities."

Teilhard describes them thusly: "On one side there are friendly and favorable forces which support our effort and steer us to success: these are the passivities of growth. On the other hand are enemy powers which sorrily interfere with our inclinations by weighing them down or detouring our path toward the super-ego, by reducing our real or apparent capacities for development. They are the passivities of reduction" (IV, 74).

Is life not the first thing we submit to, even before suffering and death? One must be able to perceive it and let it penetrate into the very depth of his self, into that place where growth springs forth: "I took the light and, by leaving the zone of my occupations and daily relationships, which was bright in appearance, I descended into the most intimate parts of myself, into the deep abyss where I confusedly felt that my power for action came from. The more I strayed from conventional evidence, which superficially illuminated my life in society, the more I realized that I was losing my sense of self. At each descending step, another person was revealed within me which I could not put an exact name to, and which no longer obeyed me. And when I had to stop my exploration, because I could no longer find the road under my feet, there appeared a bottomless pit before me, from which came a wave of unknown origin which I dare to call my life" (IV, 75).

The passivities of growth are identified with the divine presence in the deepest secrecy of the heart and human intelligence. God pursues his Creation as if through fire. Teilhard says: "To adhere to God, hidden under the interior and exterior strengths which give life and support to our being in its development, is to finally open up to and rely upon all the breaths of life" (IV, 81).

But there are also the passivities of reduction, whose numbers are great. These are the true passivities, the ones which identify themselves with death and which impede freedom. There are two types: external and internal reductions.

The external reductions, as the name indicates, are the obstacles which appear before us from everywhere: the barrier which stops the momentum, the microbe or virus which destroys little by little, an event, or an accident. These events are often unexpected and contribute to an increase of the weight of anguish on the entire life. The internal reductions form, according to Teilhard, the "blackest residue which is the most desperately useless of our lives." They are the processes of disorganization, the great psychological faults, the moral degradations, the alterations from which nothing escapes, such as old age. These passivities culminate in death, the greatest harm.

However, Christ's Resurrection is at work through all obstacles, internal and external and "the garbage of our existence can be integrated into the establishment, all around us, of the kingdom and divine milieus."

For Teilhard, thus, the spiritual life becomes a place of true realization, because it assumes the reality of a world which is in the process of fulfillment. He writes: "On a tree which had to fight against interior accidents of its development and exterior accidents of bad weather: broken branches, torn leaves, puny, dried, or faded flowers, it puts them into their proper place. They transform the growth conditions, more or less favorable, which are encountered through the trunk which supports them" (VI, 63).

But the spiritual life is also in conscious and dynamic control of the transformations and the thresholds which make up human freedom. Teilhard summarizes his point of view in a letter sent to Auguste Valensin: "I fundamentally admit that the fulfillment of the world only comes to fruition through a death, a 'night,' a reversal, a throwing off from the center and a quasi-depersonalization....The union with Christ essentially presupposes that we would realign the ultimate center of our existence to him. This would represent a radical sacrifice of egoism....However, it is absolutely necessary that Christ take up my entire life—all my life—so that I grow in Him, not only by ascetic restrictions and the supremely unifying removal of suffering, but more by everything that my existence brings about through positive efforts and natural perfection. The formula for renunciation, in order for it to be total, must satisfy these two conditions: (1) to arrange it so that we go beyond everything that is in the world; and yet, (2) to subject ourselves to pushing (with conviction and passion) the development of this same world" (IV, 100).

Suffering, physical or moral trials in their various forms,

brings into our existence this terrible battle between the forces of achievement and those of reduction. However, the hand of God has never let go of us. It is truly the rock, invisibly present at the heart of conflicts and dislocations. Teilhard ponders: "The flower that I hold has wilted in my hands, a wall has been erected before me in the curve of the road...a flame has consumed the leaf that carried my thought....The trial has arrived...and I had not definitively been sad....Why Lord? Because, in this failure of immediate supports that I risk giving to my life, I experienced, in a unique manner, that I was resting solely on your stability" (XII, 167).

This stability is perceived more and more progressively with the advance of age. The weakening of our strength changes our apparent freedom. Here, renunciation imposes itself from the exterior and progress identifies itself with the act of union to God. Prays de Chardin: "When my body (and even more my spirit) begins to show the signs of age and when evil comes upon me, whether it is from outside of myself or born within me, at that painful moment when I suddenly become conscious that I am ill or that I am aging, at this last moment, above all, when I feel that I am losing myself, absolutely passive to the hands of the great unknown forces which have molded me, at each of these dark times, my God, make it so that I understand that it is You...who is thrusting my being aside in order to penetrate all the way to the very core of my substance, in order to bring me into You" (IV, 95).

In sum, progress and detachment are one at the summit of Teilhard's mystical life.

REFLECTION QUESTIONS

How can I be attached to the world in which God placed me yet practice a high degree of detachment? Do I see in my duty to serve God through the world my own particular cross? Do I accept this cross? Do I see my work in this world as a positive and even spiritual effort? Do I hide behind a false detachment in order to cover up my lack of courage to act?

BIBLE READING

The suggested Bible reading for meditation is 2 Corinthians 12:1–10.

PRAYER

Holy Spirit, enlighten us so that we can discern the strength of God in our weakness. Amen.

DAY SEVEN
The Revealing Action

FOCUS POINT

Teilhard loved the liturgy and the feasts of the Church—Easter, Christmas, and above all, the Ascension. This feast may be seen as a metaphor of de Chardin's belief that all actions—even natural ones—can be transformed toward growth in God. As he saw it, the world is consecrated to God through the eyes of faith. Do I see all my actions as transformable in the Lord?

Earlier, because we were believers, the universe was responsible for transmitting...Jesus' actions to us. Now, because our will is righteous, it is our turn to contribute to giving Jesus his integrity through all of our actions....The greatest difficulty of our interior life is to sanely reconcile action and suffering (XII, 375).

Oh! May the time come when humankind, awakened to the meaning of the close bond which ties all the movements of this world to the unique work of the Incarnation, will not be able to address itself to any of its duties without the distinct knowledge that its work, no matter how simple, is received and used by a divine Center of the universe! At that moment, truly, few things will separate a religious life from a secular one (IV, 58).

There is no true risk in Teilhard's spirituality of dualism resulting from the fulfillment of an interior attitude through action. Action neither adds itself to, nor follows, the conviction. It is not in opposition to it, but clothes it as a garment. It is its image. Action is an adhesion, an adhesion to God. Teilhard describes it thusly: "Through the action, then, I adhere to the creative power of God. I coincide with it. Through it, I become not only an instrument but the living prolongation" (IV, 51).

The vocabulary interchanges these terms: effort, action, progress, and creation. But it does so with a view of establishing a civilization on earth without giving the impression of underestimating the collective human actions which motivate the people of our time.

In 1916, in his book *The Cosmic Life*, Teilhard had already written: "Must we dissociate ourselves from the real workings of this cosmos in order to be united with Christ?" Or again: "What then will finally be the ideal Christian, the one who is both old and new simultaneously, who will, in his soul, in his effort toward the divine Trinity, resolve the problem of the essential equilibrium by channeling all of the sap of the world?" Because the work of humans is then situated in a theological perspective, human activity could become the place of the unveiling and revelation of the true face of God.

In his *Notes to Serve the Evangelization of the New Times*, Teilhard estimates "that it is a holy and sacerdotal vocation, which is essential to the Church, for one Christian, through a passion for Christ and in order to fulfill Christ, to mingle with the workers of the world" (XII, 408). Effort and action, in spite of the difficulty that accompanies them, situates existence in both the prolongation and the perspective of Creation. In his book *My Universe*, he wrote: "The principal will of God transforms itself through the thrust of life in us....In the universe, all movements of material growth are ultimately for the spirit, and all movements of spiritual growth are ultimately for Christ....Christians must venerate and promote human effort" (IX, 95). Teilhard wanted us all to preach and practice what he called the "Gospel of Human Effort."

Assuredly, Teilhard gathered his thoughts most strongly in his book *The Divine Milieu*. There, once again, the support for his views is rigorously theological. Teilhard, making reference to Saint Paul, spelled out a sort of principal axiom: "Nothing is more certain, dogmatically, than the possible sanctification of human action" (IV, 32), which constitutes a central imperative of Christianity—the imitation of Christ in whom the Word and action are the inseparable components of religious witness. We know that for Teilhard the Incarnation is clothed in extreme importance. Should we not then consider the gospel story of the washing of the feet: "For I have set you an example, that you also should do as I have done to you" (Jn 13:15)? This reference to John's Gospel joins up with the great text of Paul to the Colossians which underlies all of Teilhard's arguments: "Above all, clothe yourselves with love, which binds everything together in perfect harmony....And whatever you do, in word or deed, do everything in the name of the Lord Jesus, giving thanks to God the Father through him" (3:14, 17).

However, Teilhard states, the deed itself, as incontestable as it may be, from the point of view of spiritual intuition, poses a problem. The problem is the time lapse between the reality of the existential plane, which is abrupt and often painful, and the eschatological interpretation that is given by faith. An initial solution reveals itself to be incomplete: human action only has value through the intention behind it. "You want…to reassert the value of your human work when your views and Christian ascetics appear to depreciate it. Oh well, inject it with the marvelous substance of good will. Purify your intentions and the least of your actions will be filled with God" (IV, 37).

The decisive solution consists of considering that all efforts must cooperate together toward the fulfillment of the world in Christ. Writes de Chardin: "Through our collaboration, which he inspires, Christ…reaches his plenitude, in every creature….Perhaps we imagine that Creation has been finished for a long time. This is an error. It continues more than ever and in the highest areas of the world….And we serve to bring it to fruition, even through the most humble works from our hands. In virtue of the interconnection of matter, soul, and Christ, no matter what we do we bring God a particle of the being that he desires" (IV, 50).

Action then permits the Christian to attain a God who calls to and attracts him, but whose attraction does not trouble or smother anything. It super-enlivens us by introducing "a superior principle of unity into our spiritual life, of which the specific effect is, according to the point of view we adopt, to sanctify human effort and humanize Christian life" (IV, 54).

Let us come back to Teilhard's view of happiness, as a follow-up to his thoughts on action and human effort. His book, *On Love and Happiness* (XI, 121), is presented in a language which is accessible to nonbelievers, and forms a realistic introductory course on the spiritual life within the dynamics of an existence that is driven by the creative breath of God. It produces what we could call three options and three conditions of personalization.

The three options correspond to three types of human beings:

- The Tired (or the pessimists), about whom Teilhard says: "For this first category, existence is an error or a failure. They are wrongly committed and as a result, it is a matter of leaving the game as skillfully as possible." Christian faith experienced in this perspective could only lead to an evasion or quitting. Here, the good seed, in all evidence, falls on the rock (see Mk 4:1–20).
- The High Livers (or the sensualists), about whom Teilhard says: "To be, to live, for the disciples of this school it is not a question of taking action but of living fully in the present moment...but for or about the future, they risk nothing." Here, faith is suffocated by the environment and these types question nothing in depth. The good seed doesn't even reach the soil.
- The Impassioneds, the final category about whom de Chardin says: "These are the ones for whom life is an ascension, a discovery. One could joke about these human beings, treat them as being naive, or find them to be a nuisance. However, it is they who have made us and it is out of them that the earth of tomorrow will emerge." Here, faith is alive and active with hope and love; it forms a credible ensemble with a vision to the Great Option which should occupy our time. The good seed has touched the soil and is buried there, certain to die, and then bring lasting fruit.

The Impassioneds climb toward the summit, but how do we get there? Teilhard proposes three conditions: "Three phases, three steps, three successive movements in the process of our interior unification, that is to say, our personalization....These three movements must necessarily correspond with the three forms of beatification."

In order to be fully himself and alive, human beings must:

- Center himself on himself: "In order to be fully ourselves, we must work throughout our entire life to organize ourselves, always bringing more order and more unity to our ideas, thoughts, and behavior. To be is, above all, to build ourselves and find ourselves."
- Decenter ourselves and focus on the Other: "There is only one Man on earth....We can only make progress toward the limits of ourselves by getting out of ourselves....From there the urgency, the deepest meaning of love...whose function and essential charm are to make us complete."
- Recenter ourselves on the Absolute: "No longer only for him to develop himself, not even only to give himself to an equal, but to submit and bring his life to something greater than himself. In other words, first of all to be, then to love, and finally to adore."

In summary, action, when understood in this way, through an attitude that comes from both humanity and interiority, is a revelation of God.

REFLECTION QUESTIONS

Are my actions in the world a reflection of the Incarnation, or am I a secret secularist? Do I see even my ordinary actions as steppingstones to Christ, or am I a pessimist whose actions are evasive and infertile? Are my actions clothed in the harmony of love, or am I suffocated by preoccupation with mindless action? Have I chosen an active and passionate life of hope and love centered on God the Absolute? If so, how do I demonstrate this fidelity?

BIBLE READING

The suggested Bible passage for meditation is John 13:1–20.

PRAYER

God of goodness, it is through our actions and convictions that we will manifest your presence to the world. Help us to act in a way that best shows you to others. Amen.

DAY EIGHT

The Spiritual Meaning of Research

FOCUS POINT

Teilhard was a great reconciler. He saw faith and science as mutually expanding each other into a larger and more sustaining vision. This larger vision included research into spiritual requirements—the means by which human beings desire to "be more," and to satisfy their search for the Absolute. Do I seek a larger vision of life?

Research is the form under which the creative power of God hides and operates most intensively in nature around us. Through our research of a new being, an additional consciousness emerges into the world.

No Christian faith is really alive if it doesn't, in its ascensional movement, reach or rise to the totality of human spiritual dynamism....The kingdom of Christ, to which we are dedicated, will only be established through either a struggle or in peace on an earth that is taken to the limit of its humanization by every pathway of technology and thought. It is through the interplay of our reason and good sense that we recognize and encounter the will of God (IX, 259).

Teilhard believed in research right down to the very depths of his Jesuit conscience. In an article entitled "About the Religious Value of Research," which he presented in Versailles in 1947 during a week-long study session organized by the Company, he proposed an answer to the question: "Why is it important for us Jesuits to participate in human research to the point of penetrating it and imprinting it on our faith and our love for Jesus?" (IX, 359).

Here, we find the double and inseparate requirement of the "above" and the "ahead." Christian faith can only question the contemporary world if it contrasts the two components of a complete "humano-Christian mysticism." The adoration of God cannot arouse the suspicion of the world. Research about the kingdom cannot be put into conflict with research about the energies of Creation. Prayer does not exclude knowledge, even if it infinitely transcends it.

"It is vain...and unjust to pit science against Christ," wrote de Chardin, "or to separate them as if they are two areas which are strangers to each other. Science alone cannot discover Christ, but it is Christ who fulfills the desires which are born in our hearts in the science classroom" (IX, 62).

It is precisely because of this articulation between different elements, indeed, the necessary unity and complementarity between these two perspectives of research, that Teilhard opposed the sterilizing separation of the various levels or points of view.

Right from the beginning, his thinking was multi-disciplinary. At that point and at that same time, one finds both de Chardin's richness and his difficulty. It is through his clear-sightedness in confronting and uniting in the same quest for meaning the great experimental and symbolic interpretations of the world that made Teilhard a true innovator.

Thus, we can speak of a great plan for reconciliation between science and faith, between the Church and the modern world. Says de Chardin: "Yes, I would like to reconcile God with what is good in the modern world: its scientific intuitions, its social appetites, its legitimate criticisms." And Teilhard put himself to the task, starting from the point of his own scholarly ability. One can resolutely believe in God as well as the world in the same action. To adore "the One who will come" with as much conviction as we have confidence in science in order to help unravel the complexity of the world which is constantly evolving.

Already in 1933 de Chardin was concerned: "The idea is widespread...that religions express a primitive and outmoded state of humanity. Science, by discovering the experimental explanation of these same phenomena, has rendered God and religions useless. That is the credo of many of our contemporaries. It is greatly important to react against this narrow manner of understanding the birth and history of the idea of God in the world" (IX, 131).

In the convergent universe which is revealed by science, Christ finds plenitude in his creative action. The religious conscience, not to say mystical experience, is in no way hindered by scientific observations and conclusions. If there is reciprocal calling into question, it is done with respect to order and finalities: experimental for science, symbolic for religion; and may the dialogue that is opened between the two permit an extension of their respective domains. In this sense, science crosses over, more and more, to the symbolic field; and the religious or faith point of view extends itself to the global reality of the universe.

The two steps are not mutually exclusive and must unite themselves, not only on the objective basis of research but in the interior of each person who questions himself about his own life and about universal destiny.

We must be both scientific and a believer with the same attitude of faith, a synthesis of experience and adhesion, of techniques and love. Teilhard is suspicious of spiritual and cultural "schizophrenia" which awaits us when we want to establish separations and impassable barriers between the various registers of our existence.

"'Be scientific in peace without getting yourself mixed up in philosophy or theology'—that is the advice (and warning) that the authorities would have repeated to me during my life. That is still, I imagine, the directions given to the numbers of brilliant trainees who are thrown today, very fortunately, into the realm of research. But it is also the attitude about which, respectfully—with the assurance I have gained in over fifty years spent at the heart of the problem—I would like to make the remark, to whom it may concern, that it is psychologically unlivable and, in addition, directly contrary to the greater glory of God" (IX, 283).

These lines introduce the last pages sent by Teilhard before his death. They are titled in a significant way: "Research, Work, and Adoration." In this document, which perfectly sums up the battle of his entire life, Teilhard saw three aspects.

The first aspect is the realization that, parallel to the progress of scientific research, humanity has developed a desire to live better and to "be more." The scientific spirit and faith in the "before" are in agreement: "A researcher, who is worthy of the name, can no longer work unless supported by the idea of pushing the limit, and pushing the world around him to the very end. In other words, at the very least, all researchers today have functionally become 'believers in the before,' and fans of the 'ultrahuman.'"

The second aspect is a consequence. Don't consider science as an addition or an accessory to the kingdom, but accept a rethinking of the religious vision by observing that the discovery of a world in evolution does not diminish the Christian spirit but reinforces it "all the way to the highest expression of itself."

The third aspect is a practical device. Teilhard asks that there be specialized religious training for researchers and future researchers. This would necessarily involve a further deepening of the very notion of Christian perfection right from the time that they are taken to the new world of laboratories and factories where "the old opposition of earth and heaven disappears (or is amended) in favor of a new formula: "to heaven by the fulfillment of earth."

Each modern religious crisis is born out of an apparent conflict between the neo-humanistic mysticism of a "before" and the Christian mysticism of the "above." The Christian approach is a reconciliation, not on the surface, but organically, of these two currents, the one with the other. We could fear the difficulty and paradoxes inherent in this task, but the credibility of the Church in the modern world depends solely upon it.

Teilhard has promised: "I am going to try to make you love science in a Christian manner by establishing the following two propositions: The scientific study of the world...essentially analytical, makes us walk backwards from divine realities; but, on the other hand...by revealing to us the synthetic structure of the world, it throws us, by its natural prolongation, toward the unique Center of things, which is God our Lord" (IX, 47).

For Teilhard, research includes the vast domain of ethics. He considered ethical requirements, under the multitudinous forms they must take, as the way to fulfillment and as a means to "be more" for man. In the history of evolution, thought, research, and ethics are indissolubly bound. Teilhard remarks: "It is impossible to concretely push beyond a certain degree of progress in human sciences without this power of reflected arrangement automatically coming from internal obligations...at the same time as it engenders a totally new atmosphere of spiritual requirements" (V, 262).

Teilhard pleaded, on account of the non-opposition between the gospel and science, for an "ethic of movement," answering to both the constant attraction to Christ and the tentative research of humanity. All the classical dimensions of ethics (equilibrium, money, love, individual, social) are maintained but transformed into a dynamic meaning to give an explanation about the sprouting forth of life and the creative energy that flows through beings and humanity.

He said: "The world will construct itself finally through moral strengths and moral reciprocity as a function of building the world. A whole new appreciation is leading to a renewed program of ethics" (VI, 131).

The spiritual meaning of research will come from the fact that it manifests the inscription and the indication of the God of love in the world in its experimental perspectives as much as in its moral dimensions.

REFLECTION QUESTIONS

Am I a believer in a religion of progress and technology divorced from its spiritual roots, or can I find a God of "all things" and even "small things"? Do I cultivate and nurture moral strength through both reason and reliance on God's stability? Do I look for something better than the corrupt and even boring aspects of the modern world? Am I a reconciler in my own heart and in the hearts of the people around me?

BIBLE READING

The suggested Bible reading for meditation is Matthew 25:14–30.

PRAYER

Jesus, with your help, arrange it so that we will be men and women of the future, with no fear of progress. Amen.

DAY NINE
The Spiritual Power of Matter

FOCUS POINT

For Tielhard, the Incarnation symbolizes the human face of God while his Revelation is disclosed to the hearts of all believers—surely a very high expression of the spiritual unity of matter and the basis of our affiliation with all the members of Christ's body. In de Chardin's view, matter becomes the support for God's Revelation and Christ's Incarnation. Do I see and acknowledge a world imbued with Christ's presence?

Finally, I put myself to the task of writing something—in a semi-poetic style—in an allegorical form. The allegory is the story of Elijah: "While they continued walking and talking, a chariot of fire and horses of fire separated the two of them, and Elijah ascended in a whirlwind into heaven" (2 Kings 2:11).

You understand that the whirlwind is the matter that draws and liberates those who know how to grasp spiritual power (GDP, 390).

Our goal for this ninth day—similar to the one for the twelfth day—is to allow ourselves to meditate exclusively on Teilhard's text in all its unity and beauty.

We will proceed in this way: first, a few explanations will be given about the significance of matter to Teilhard; then a passage from the biblical text that inspired his hymn to the universe will be set down; and, finally, Teilhard's written allegory on the nature of matter will be presented.

We can approach matter, observes Teilhard, only by considering the creative union "that established a direct relationship between the spirituality of the soul and the complexity of the body and discovered, by the very act, a precise relationship between quality and quantity. There is no spiritual unity without the principle of a unifying power" (XII, 202).

There is no similarity between spirit and matter but no opposition either. Matter, in the creative breath of God, is a paradoxically fragile place of manifold features and an illumination owing to its spiritual end. Ambiguity and power, obscurity and light characterize this fundamental reality which can only be understood through a movement that ties ascendence and interiorization together. It is like the flesh of Christ in which the eternal Word is written. Matter is the support for God's revelation and contemplation.

Teilhard's "Hymn of the Universe" constitutes the end of the text entitled *The Spiritual Power of Matter*. In its entirety, this work is a lyrical and symbolic meditation, beginning with the text from the second book of Kings. The prophet Elijah, by enabling his disciple Elisha to withstand the hardship of his departure, made him understand that the true prophetical sign is a vision. That which is hidden to human beings is revealed to the prophet who sees the presence and actions of God through events: "The more I press on the entire surface of reality, the more I will also attain Christ and tightly hug myself to him. God, the eternal being in him, is everywhere, one could say, in the process of formation for us. And God is also the heart of everything" (XIII, 80).

Teilhard gives a mystical reading of a prophetic text. The spiritual life allows access to the invisible so that certain people see what others do not. Does Teilhard compare himself to Elisha? Probably. We can then understand the final lines of his last book, *Le Christique* (The Christic), written shortly before his death: "How then did it happen that, looking around me, and still exalted by what I had seen, I find myself virtually alone, one of a kind, alone to have seen? How is it that I am not able, when they ask me, to cite a single author or a single book where the marvelous 'transparency,' which in my eyes has transformed everything, is recognized and clearly explained. And how is it that, 'descended from the mountain,' and in spite of the magnificence that I see with my own eyes, I find myself so little bettered, so little pacified, and so little capable of communicating to others through my actions the marvelous unity into which I feel myself plunged?" (XIII, 115).

But even facing this hesitation, the certainty of the inner truth was brought home to him, and Teilhard, in an appendix to *The Heart of Matter* (written in 1950), repeated the "Hymn of the Universe" from 1919 and noted that this text always transmitted the depth of his thoughts.

Here is the story of Elijah from the second book of Kings that Teilhard used to reveal his own in-depth meditations on matter:

> When they had crossed, Elijah said to Elisha, "Tell me what I may do for you, before I am taken from you." Elisha said, "Please let me inherit a double share of your spirit." He responded, "You have asked a hard thing; yet, if you see me as I am being taken from you, it will be granted you; if not, it will not." As they continued walking and talking, a chariot of fire and horses of fire separated the two of them, and Elijah ascended in a whirlwind into heaven. Elisha kept watching and crying out, "Father, father! The chariots of Israel and its horsemen!" But when he could no longer see him, he grasped his own clothes and tore them into two pieces. He picked up the mantle of Elijah that had fallen from him, and went back and stood at the bank of the Jordan (2 Kings 2:9–13).

Here is de Chardin's extended reflection on the nature of spirit and matter which he based on the story of Elijah:

> The Man fell to his knees in the chariot of fire which carried him.
>
> And he said this: "Blessed are you, harsh matter, sterile sod, hard rock, you who only cede to violence and who forces us to work if we want to eat.
>
> "Blessed are you, dangerous Matter, violent sea, uncontrollable passion, you who devour us if we fetter you.
>
> "Blessed are you, powerful matter, irresistible evolution, ever-renewing reality, you who would, at any moment, burst our restraints, you force us to pursue the truth even further.
>
> "Blessed are you, universal matter, duration without limits, ether without shores, triple abyss of the stars,

atoms and generations, you who reveal the dimensions of God to us by overflowing and dissolving our narrow measures.

"Blessed are you, impenetrable matter, you who, spread out everywhere between our souls and the world of essential beings, make us languish in the desire to pierce the seamless veil of phenomena.

"Blessed are you, mortal matter, you who, by disassociating from us one day, will by force introduce us to the very heart of the one who is.

"Without you, matter, without your attacks, without your removals, we would live inert, stagnant, puerile, ignorant of ourselves and of God. You who murder and you who feed, you who resist and you who bend, you who upset and you who build, you who bind in chains and you who liberate; you, sap of our souls, hand of God, flesh of Christ, matter, I bless you.

"I bless and hail you matter, you, not as you are described, reduced, or disfigured by the pontiffs of science or the preachers of virtue—a gathering, they say, of brutal forces or base appetites—but the one who appears to me today, in your entirety and your truth.

"Hail, matter, inexhaustible capacity of being and transformation where the chosen substance germinates and grows.

"Hail, matter, universal power of reconciliation and union, by which the crowd of monads join together and in which they all converge on the path to the Spirit.

"Hail, matter, harmonious totality of souls, limpid crystal from which the new Jerusalem is drawn.

"Hail, matter, Divine Milieu, charged with creative power, ocean agitated by the Spirit, clay kneaded and given life through the incarnate Word.

"By believing that they are obeying your irresistible call, man often rushes out of love to you in the exterior abyss of egoistical pleasures. A reflection or an echo fools them.

"Now I see it. In order to reach you, matter, one must be part of a universal contact with everything that moves here down below; we feel that the particular forms of all that we are holding is fading in our hands until we stay at grips with the only essence of all consistencies and unions.

"We must, if we are to have you, sublimate you in pain after having seized you voluptuously in our arms.

"You reign, matter, in the heights where the saints imagine themselves avoiding you—flesh so transparent and so mobile that we can no longer distinguish you from a spirit.

"Take me away there above, matter, through effort, separation, and death—take me away there where it will be possible finally to chastely embrace the universe!"

Down below, on the desert which has returned to tranquillity, someone cried: "My Father, my Father! What foolish wind has carried you away!"

And on the ground lies a mantle.

REFLECTION QUESTIONS

Do I long to inherit the spirit of the Lord as does Elisha? Have I been seduced by the irresistible pleasures of an ego deprived of the spirit of love? Am I a true member of Christ's body, a diffuser of love in the community of saints, a harmonious influence on the totality of the souls? Is my spiritual life stagnant and tired, or can I find a way to mobilize the energy of love?

BIBLE READING

The suggested Bible reading for meditation is John 1:1–18.

PRAYER

Holy Spirit, you make us contemplate the indelible traces of the infinite God in the world and in humanity. Amen.

DAY TEN
The Priest

FOCUS POINT

Teilhard brought the fact of his priesthood into the secular arenas of science and into the killing fields of battle (as a stretcher-bearer in World War I). He saw all callings as apostleships for Jesus Christ, and he saw adoration of God the Omega as an essential part of any vocation. Have I united my work solidly to the mission and love of Christ, or is it a compartmentalized part of my existence?

My God, to encourage your action throughout everything in me, I will do more than open and offer myself to the passivities of existence. I will faithfully associate myself with your work on my body and soul. I will force myself to follow and anticipate your smallest impulses. Oh, if I could resist you so little, Master, that you will no longer distinguish me from You!

Within the limits of my powers, because I am a priest, I want to be, from now on, the first to be aware of what the world loves, follows, and suffers—the first to seek, to sympathize, and to grieve—the first to blossom and to sacrifice myself—in the broadest human way and with more earthly nobility than any other servant of the world (XII, 325).

Teilhard was a true priest and faithful to his profound mission right to the end. Father d'Ouince said, at a memorial service which was celebrated in Paris: "Few sacerdotal existences have been, I think, so totally unified" (HDL, 371). This aspect of his personality had not perhaps been evoked enough. The mystical dimension of his work and of his personality, determined by the alliance within himself of the scholar and the religious, never diminished for an instant the radical nature of his personal gift to Christ. The gift made him not only a man with an unsettling interiority but also one of great generosity. He was a true disciple and apostle of Christ even in the simplest of circumstances.

The mission to which the young priest (ordained in 1911) felt himself called was equal only to his personal search and his great thirst for the Absolute. The first aspect is truly in the grand tradition of the Church, the work of salvation, but carried to infinite dimensions. Teilhard wrote: "Jesus, all priest and because a priest, dedicated his life to the work of universal salvation. If a priest is conscious of his dignity, he should no longer live for himself, but for the world, following the example of the One whom he is anointed to represent. Jesus, it seems that this task takes on a more immediate urgency and a more precise significance for me than for others who are much better than myself. The nuances of your calling are innumerable! How essentially diverse are the vocations! Each region, nation, and social category have had their own apostles. I would like to be, Lord, in my humble way, an apostle and an evangelist for your Christ in the Universe" (XII, 322).

Teilhard was profoundly a priest from the very depths of his being to the outer tensions of the world. He first realized this fact during the great war of 1914 when he lived in a state of total dedication to others, refusing all promotions. The terrible experience of World War I is at the same time a rupture and an intensified communion with the God of Creation and fulfillment. In such a context, the priest becomes a revealer of the birth of another world, all the way into the pain of combat. Teilhard cries: "Oh priests who are in the war...you have the power—through your ordination—to consecrate, in a real way and through the flesh and blood of Christ, the sufferings that surround you, and in which your priestly character orders you to participate.

"You have never been more a priest than now, mixed up and submerged...in the sorrows and the blood of a generation—never more active—never more directly in the line of your vocation" (XII, 332).

Teilhard would remain a Jesuit through his research and throughout his entire scholarly life. He brought into a setting which was often anti-clerical a witness of great intellectual and spiritual truth by manifesting a profound respect for the ideas and convictions of others. All the while he made the Christian faith accessible and credible for a great number of men and women who were, in fact, far removed from the Church in their knowledge or their positivist prejudices.

He said: "Is the priest not the one who must carry the weight of life, and show by his actions how one could unite human work with the love of God? (GDP, 238)....Is it really true, then, Lord, that by spreading science and freedom, I am able to concentrate on these as well as to plunge myself into the divine atmosphere which is my greatest single desire?" (HU, 124).

The priest, at the same time, lives the dual necessity of both apostolate and adoration, work in the world and the work of love which alone can explain the folly of his total offering. Teilhard points out that, in his ministry, the priest can realize the mystery of the Incarnation: "Through the Incarnation, you realize the triple dream of love in the unbelievable plenitude: (1) to wrap yourself in the loved Object until you are drowned there; (2) to endlessly intensify his presence there; and, (3) to lose yourself there without ever being satiated....May the temporary and circumspect contact with sacramental things introduce me to a universal and perpetual communion with Christ, his omni-active will and his mystically illuminated Body" (XII, 327).

Teilhard never dissociated his personal priesthood from his long, multifaceted quest for truth. The world in its multitude and maturity is present in de Chardin's offertory prayer: "One by one, I see and love those which you have given to me like a natural charm of my existence. One by one...I count the members of this other and equally dear family that the affinities of the heart and scientific research and thought have gathered, little by little, around me, from the most dissimilar elements. More confusingly, but all without exception, I evoke those members of the anonymous troupe which make up the innumerable mass of the living, that is, those who surround and support me without me even knowing them; those who come and those who go; those, above all, who in truth or by error, at their desks, laboratories, or factories, believe in the progress of things and passionately pursue the light today" (HDU, 18).

An aspect to which we return to by evoking the Church is Teilhard's personal faithfulness to his religious and sacerdotal commitment, a commitment unquestionably supported by his profound and constant relationship with the risen Christ. He prays: "Oh Lord, I want my acceptance to always be more complete, wider, and more intense! May my being present itself always as more open and more transparent to your influence! And may I, in this way, feel your action always closer, your presence always more dense, everywhere around me. *Fiat, Fiat*" (XII, 325).

His faithfulness to his ordination promises were kept, without fail, all throughout a life of upheaval which was often draining and in spite of innumerable exterior solicitations and pressures of all kinds to which he was subjected. At the end of his life he said: "This faithfulness did not require a struggle that I remember. I could love only Christ."

But "to take everything into account," stated René d'Ouince, "the dominant trait of Father Teilhard's personality seems to me to be his unalterable kindness. He, so frugal with his time, like all the great workers, was ready to give time to whoever came to consult him: a student, a novice, or an older lady who endlessly questioned him." The man always stayed faithful to his youthful intuition from which, even more, his sacerdotal responsibility had its roots: "If I acquired a conviction...it was that, in relationships with others, we should never think we are too good or too gentle; gentleness is the first of our strengths and perhaps the first virtue among those that we see in ourselves" (GDP, 67).

How can we not cite the paradoxical adventurer and writer, Henry de Monfreid here, through his rendering to his "travel companion" to the Red Sea (Teilhard), quoting the most beautiful homage there is: "Nobody could avoid this sublime influence, and the worst would become better, rehabilitated in their own eyes by the generous confidence that he accorded them, this man who knew how to look to the darkest corners of their souls, not to judge them, but to discover the latent virtues there, to make unexpected reflection spring forth from this shadow, like the spark of a diamond, lost in the impurity, that all of a sudden shines in the ray of a star. How many unhappy, discouraged people, who were bitter and upset...how many of these outcasts, perverted and lost through their own self-scorn have been comforted and saved by this man with a limpid glance, who knew how to give new life to dead consciences, like Jesus of Nazareth raised up Lazarus from the dead?"

The scholar and the priest were never in conflict. The researcher and the mystic completed each other in service to the single mission of the Church which Teilhard always understood at its widest angle. He comments: "It is good to spread the kingdom of God to new peoples. But it is better and more direct to make it penetrate to the very heart of humanity. If we succeeded in implanting the love of Jesus Christ into this precise point, we will be surprised to see the people who spontaneously flow towards Jerusalem" (EP, 67).

REFLECTION QUESTIONS

Do I follow—and even anticipate—the smallest signs of God's intentions for me? Do I see myself as only preoccupied with my own personal salvation or does my mission include being a servant of the world as well? Have I helped spread the kingdom of God to the heart of humanity, or am I one whose silence is a form of denial? Do I see gentleness as strength and one of the first of the virtues? Do I say "Let it be" with sincerity, or do I have a small streak of manipulatory ego that challenges God's plans for me?

BIBLE READING

The suggested Bible reading for meditation is John 21:15–19.

PRAYER

All-powerful God, give priests to your Church so that it will be a sign and source of salvation. Amen.

DAY ELEVEN

The Eucharist, an Ardent Meeting Point

FOCUS POINT

Tony Kelly, noted Redemptorist theologian, writes: "In a world threatened with ecological disintegration and cultural uprootedness from nature, the eucharist nourishes faith into a gracious, ultimate wholeness." Teilhard, likewise, saw the Eucharist as a transforming agent, gathering the Church into a great communion in which the individual and the universal plan of salvation were united.

In reality, among the sacraments, the Eucharist stands apart from the others. It is the first of the sacraments, or more exactly, it is the only sacrament to which the others refer. And this is for good reason since, through it, the axis of the Incarnation directly passes, that is to say, the axis of Creation (X, 194).

When the priest says these words: "This is my Body," the words fall directly on the bread and directly transform it into the individual reality of Christ. But the great sacramental operation does not stop at this local and temporary event....Beyond the life of each man, and all of the ages of the Church, and all of the periods of the world, there is only one Mass and only one Communion (IV, 151).

In his spiritual life and all the way through Teilhard's scientific research, the Eucharist occupied an essential place. The faith of this Jesuit scholar was imminently eucharistic. We can understand devotion to the extent that—supported by all the theological tradition of Christianity—he considered this sacrament to be the sign *par excellence* of God's presence in the world. Father Teilhard felt that eucharistic communion had consequences that greatly surpassed sensory limits, or the time and space where we live our faith. He wrote: "My God, when I approach the altar to take communion, arrange it so that I understand even more deeply the infinite hidden perspectives under the smallness and closeness of the host where you hide yourself. Already I am used to recognizing, under the inertia of this piece of bread, a devouring power that, by following the expressions of your greatest Doctors, assimilates me—a far cry from letting itself be assimilated by me.... In the host, it is my life that you are offering to me, Jesus" (IV, 154).

The Eucharist, in Teilhard's mystical vision, is at the very center, not only of the spiritual life but of the life of the world—through the mystery of the invisible Church—and of the irreversible evolution of the world. It is not amazing that it would be in *The Divine Milieu* that we would meet the strongest passages concerning the Eucharist, which constitute, in a certain way, the soul of the divine milieu.

Teilhard progressively leads us to the discovery of this center through which God keeps us in the field of his presence. It is the Universal Christ that transforms us and gathers us in a great communion. The traditional notion of the Mystical Body takes back then its whole dimension on the condition of understanding the invisible and universal significance of the Eucharist. For Teilhard, the great sacramental operation does not stop with the local and temporary event.

He points out: "Truly, since the origins of the messianic preparations until the second coming of Christ at the end of time...a single event has developed in the world: the Incarnation, realized in each person through the Eucharist. All of the communions of a life form a single communion. All the communions of all the people who are living form a single communion. All the communions of all mankind—past, present, and future form a single communion" (IV, 151).

The Eucharist is the brilliant and ardent meeting place which attests, in the very heart of history and of each individual's history, to the transcendent faithfulness of the universal plan of salvation. It puts into action God's creative and recapitulative dynamism. Gustave Martelet explained what this meant: "Often, one must say it, we have remained captive of a vision of a eucharistic presence which is too limited in its effects to only the sacrament. Teilhard showed us that a transubstantiation that imprisoned faith in 'species' had, quite to the contrary, enlarged it. He has thus opened the world to eucharistic 'extensions' and has contributed to making it understood that we must start from the Resurrection in order to grasp the true mystery of the Divine Presence."

For the Christ who is present is truly the risen Christ, equal to the expectations of the world. The world is thirsty for adoration. The more humans develop, the more they will feel the need to adore. And Teilhard prayed: "Oh Jesus, pierce the clouds with your lightning! Show yourself to us as the Strong One, the Brilliance, the Arisen! Be to us the Pantocrator who occupies the full solitude of the cupolas in the old basilicas! We need nothing less than this second coming of Christ at the end of time to equilibrate and dominate the glory of the rising world in our hearts" (IV, 158).

Here, Teilhard reaches, once again, the point of view of the "Meditation on Christ's Kingdom" found in Saint Ignatius' *Spiritual Exercises*: "To see Christ our Lord, eternal king, and before him, the whole universe which he calls, at the same time as he calls each person in particular, by saying: my will is to conquer the entire world...and thus to enter into the glory of my Father."

The Eucharist reminds us that the kingdom is within ourselves. However, the kingdom is called to develop itself within us. The milieu of love can and must grow. It is then necessary to be truly conscious of the presence of God which resembles a breeze much more than a hurricane. God's presence, signified in Communion, can manifest itself in an insignificant transformation of a glance or the heart, by a taste of the being, the discovery of a profound modification of things, or an intuition of the infinite. This presence effectively realizes that which, up until then, could not be—and still is, for many—only simple intuition.

Writes de Chardin: "A breeze passes in the night. When did it come up? Where did it come from? Where is it going? No one knows. No one can force the spirit, the glance, the light of God to come to him. One day, man becomes aware that he has become sensitive to a certain perception of the divine which has spread everywhere. Ask him about it. When did this begin for him? He won't be able to tell. All that he will know is that a new spirit has crossed his life" (IV, 159).

The Eucharist transforms the life of a Christian by incorporating him again even more closely with his Master. Teilhard spoke of the "enveloping embrace" of Christ. In spite of the fragile aspects of the sacramental rite, its contingencies and historic variables, that which happens in the eucharistic act truly brings the words of Christ back together with the discourse about the bread of life: "Those who eat my flesh and drink my blood abide in me, and I in them. Just as the living Father sent me, and I live because of the Father, so whoever eats me will live because of me" (Jn 6:56–57).

Teilhard points out: "In me, periodically, the saintly species will blossom. Each time, they leave me more profoundly ensconced into the great expanse of your Omni-presence: living or dying, I will never stop, at any time, advancing within you" (IV, 155).

The sacrament of the divine presence should not be confused with the simple human or social bond to the community nor even with baptism, which is the sign of entry into the Church. There is much more here; there is a veritable union through the center point and, equally, there is a physical experience, as de Chardin describes: "Christ could not consummate our unity in the center, which is fixed above us, from his Spirit, unless he had previously enclosed us in a material network upheld by our 'corporeal being.' In order to be the Soul of our souls, it is necessary that he begin by being the Flesh of our flesh."

But when we take Communion, we never appropriate the living Christ for ourselves. At the instant when we think we are enclosing the Divine Presence, it seems to escape us and draws us constantly forward. Communion, while bringing us closer to God through the body of his Son, opens our perspectives about the world and about others. It doesn't hold us but puts us on the road by situating God always up ahead, like the

One who calls us to go to him by traversing the world and by loving our neighbors. Father Pierre reflects: "No matter how thin the Host is, I lose myself in it without succeeding in grasping it or coinciding with it. Its center flees even while attracting me....As I thought I was enclosing it, it was not the Host I was holding, but one of the thousand creatures in the midst of which my life is entangled: a suffering, a joy, a job, a brother to console or to love" (HU, 155).

The text that we will read in the following chapter will unfold, in a poetic, but nevertheless, in a realistic manner, the significance of the Eucharist in the life of the world. What is certain is that Teilhard placed this sacrament as "the source and the summit of Christian life." Later, the Second Vatican Council would remind us of the Eucharist's full dimension and its singular place in the nature of being Christian as well as its spiritual responsibility in the Church today.

"Between men and me, you would, with the help of your Eucharist, manifest the fundamental attraction (already felt obscurely in all types of intense love) that mysteriously transforms a myriad of reasoning creatures into a similar type of monad (unit) in you, Jesus Christ" (HU, 98).

REFLECTION QUESTIONS

Do I make a point of nourishing the kingdom of God within myself by uniting myself to the universal plan of salvation through my reception of the Eucharist? Am I aware of the "enveloping embrace" of Christ when I consume the Eucharist? Am I aware of being "more fully at one" with the presence of God during the Eucharist?

BIBLE READING

The suggested Bible reading for meditation is John 6:22–59.

PRAYER

Lord Jesus, you are the living bread descended from heaven, the one who deeply nourishes our faith. Amen.

DAY TWELVE

Mass on the Altar of the World

FOCUS POINT

God, who is "both further than everything and deeper than everything," is immediately present to us in the Mass, in the body and blood of Jesus Christ. And it *is* Christ, and those members of His Body—the Church—who consume Him in the Eucharist, who bring about the gradual transformation of the world, wherein all things are brought into unity with Christ.

When I travel by mule for entire days...I repeat—for want of other masses—the "Mass on the Altar of the World" that you know, and I believe that I say it with more lucidity and conviction than before (LLZ, 46).

In praying, I always elaborate, little by little, my "mass about things." It seems that, in a way, the true substance to conse-

crate daily, is the growth of the world for that day—the bread symbolizing very well what creation produces, the wine (blood) representing the weariness and suffering it eliminates through its effort (LDV, 46).

Teilhard's "Mass on the Altar of the World" (XIII, 139) is, without a doubt, the text that is the most well known, the one which has been edited and translated the most.

Without signifying the entirety of Teilhard's thoughts, this work, composed in a lyrical and carefully mastered poetic style, is a long prayer whose main theme is divided into five sections. This prayer represents the illuminated and active presence of God in the world. This presence is perfectly signified in the Christian rite of the Eucharist, where the priest, in the name of Christ, is the celebrant.

This is a text of a mystical nature, an affirmative meditation rather than a logical analysis, the expression of a vision and of an interior certainty rather than the transmission of a tradition or knowledge.

Written in its primary form during the war in 1918 and first entitled "The Priest," it was reworked in 1923 and appears as we know it now. Its structure is the same as that of the Eucharist: Offertory (Offertory of the Mass), The Fire Above the World (Preface and Invocation of the God of Majesty), The Fire in the World (Invocation of the Spirit Which Descends Upon the Offerings), Communion (Communion of the Faithful), and, finally, Prayer (Concluding Prayer). In the following sections, we will meditate on this text through some of its essential passages.

OFFERTORY

In the first of the five sections, Teilhard writes:

> Since, once again, Lord, no longer in the forests of Aisne, but in the Asian steppes, I have neither bread, nor wine, nor an altar, I lift myself up over the symbols, all the way to the pure majesty of reality. I will offer to you, as your priest, on the altar of the entire earth, the work and the sorrows of the world.
>
> The sun just rose beyond and illuminates the extreme fringes of the Orient. Once more, under the moving cover of the sun's fires, the living surface of the earth awakens, trembles, and begins its awesome labor again.
>
> Oh my God, I will place the expected harvest of this new effort onto my paten. Into my chalice, I will pour the sap of all the fruit which will, today, be crushed.
>
> My chalice and my paten are the depths of a soul which is widely opened to all the forces which, in an instant, are going to lift themselves from all points of the globe and converge toward the Spirit. May the memory and the mystical presence of those who have been awakened by the light for a new day then come to me!...
>
> Lord, receive this complete host which Creation, moved by your attraction, presents to you in the new dawn. This bread, our effort, is on its own, but an immense disintegration. This wine, our pain, alas, is nothing but a dissolving beverage. But at the heart of this formless mass, you have placed—I am sure of it because I feel it—an irresistible and sanctifying desire which makes us cry out, from the impious right to the faithful: "Lord, make us one!"

Because, in the absence of spiritual zeal and the sublime purity of your saints, my God, you have given me an irresistible sympathy for everything that moves within obscure matter—because, immediately, I recognize much more than a child of heaven, a son of the earth, in myself—this morning, I will climb, in thought, to the high places, filled with my mother's hopes and miseries; and there—strengthened with a ministry that you alone, I believe, have given me—upon everything that appears about to be born or perish, in human flesh, under the sun that rises, I will call fire.

THE FIRE ABOVE THE WORLD

In the second section of "The Mass on the Altar of the World," Father Pierre writes:

> We are dominated by the tenacious illusion that fire, this principle of being, comes from the depths of the earth and that its flame progressively lights itself along the brilliant wake of life. Lord, you have given me the grace to understand that this vision is a false one and in order to perceive you, I must rid myself of it. At the beginning, there was intelligent, loving, and active strength. At the beginning, there was the Word which was supremely capable of subjecting to itself and manipulating any matter that could be born. At the beginning, there was no cold or shadows; there was Fire. That is the Truth....Burning spirit, fundamental and personal fire, the real end of a union that is a thousand times more beautiful and desirable than the destructive fusion that is imagined by any pantheism, deem, once again, to descend to present a soul on the frail

skin of new matter which is going to envelope the world....

Sparkling Word, ardent strength, you who work the multiple in order to breathe your life into it, I beg you, lower your powerful hands, your kind hands, your omni-present hands on us, those hands which touch neither here nor there but which, blended with the present and past depth and the universe of things, simultaneously reach out to us by all that is the most vast and the most interior, in us and around us."

THE FIRE IN THE WORLD

In this third section, Teilhard writes about the invocation of the spirit. He records these words:

It is done. Once again, the Fire has penetrated the Earth. It did not fall loudly on the summits, like the lightning in its bolt. Does the Master force open his own doors when he comes home?

Without a tremor, without thunder, the flame illuminated everything from within. From the heart of the tiniest atom right to the energy of the most universal laws, it naturally invaded each element, both individually and together...each liaison of our Cosmos, so that we could believe it inflamed itself spontaneously....

Now Lord, through the consecration of the world, in my eyes, the glimmer and the perfume floating through the universe assume a body and face through you. What my hesitant thought caught a glimpse of, and what reclaimed my heart, asked for through an improbable desire, you give to me magnificently. May the creatures not only be so interdependent among

> themselves so that not one of them could exist without all the others around them, but may they be so suspended in the same real center, that a veritable Life, lived in common, give them their persistence and union....
>
> If I cannot believe that your true Presence gives life, softens and reheats the least of the energies which penetrate and touch me lightly, is it that, chilled to the core of my being, I have not died from the cold?

COMMUNION

In the fourth section which commemorates communion, de Chardin writes:

> If Fire has descended to the heart of the World, it is finally to take and absorb me. From then on, it is not enough for me to contemplate it, and that through constant faith, I endlessly intensify its ardor around me. It is necessary, after having cooperated with all my strength in the consecration that makes it spring forth, that I finally consent to the communion that will give to it, in my person, the food that it has finally come to seek.
>
> I bow down, my God, before your presence in the universe which has become ardent and, under the guise of all that I will meet and all that will happen to me and all that I will accomplish in this day, I want you and I wait for you....
>
> The world can only finally join you, Lord, through a type of inversion, a reversal and offsetting where not only individual accomplishments, but the very appearance of all human advantages disappear for a while. So

that my being will be decidedly annexed to yours, it is necessary that, within myself, the world dies...that is to say that I must pass through the agonizing phase of reduction where nothing tangible comes as compensation. That is why, by retreating into the chalice of the bitterness of all separations, of all limitations, of all sterile forfeitures, you hand it to me saying: "Drink all of it."

REFLECTION QUESTIONS

Do I consider myself an active part in the divine plan to transform all things into unity with Christ? In what ways can I help to bring about the development of humanity to this end?

BIBLE READING

The suggested Bible reading for meditation is Acts 2.

PRAYER

You, the Spirit of God, transform our lives, our sorrows and our joys into the body and blood of Christ. Amen.

DAY THIRTEEN
Believe in the Church

FOCUS POINT

The Church is the Body of Christ, a communion between God and Man. The Church is our anchor, a stabilizing force that encourages, nurtures, and provides for our spiritual needs. An evolving body, the Church is in process, its pilgrim people striving for deeper union with God.

I believe in the Church that mediates between God and the world, and I love it. It seems that it gives me a great deal of peace....I hope, with God's help, to never do anything against the Church, apart from which I discern no course of life with a chance to succeed (ER, 504).

A type of ultra-socialization is in progress: the one by which "the Church" is taking shape, little by little, giving life through its influence to all the spiritual energies of the noosphere (de Chardin's name for the envelope of thinking consciousness that covers the earth), and collecting them under their most sublime form. The Church is the portion of the world which is reflexively Christified, the principal focus point of interhuman affinities through super-charged charity. The Church is the central axis of universal convergence and the precise point of effervescent meeting between the universe and the Omega point (IX, 206).

The Church meant a great deal to Teilhard, and we remain much too circumspect on this point. The undeniable difficulties of the Jesuit with his order and the institutional Church—of which we know the contextual reasons—must not make us forget his love of the Church and his will to never be separated from it. For him, the Church was the Body of Christ, and it was unthinkable for him, even when he was in great difficulty, to distance himself for a single moment from the spiritual, human, and social communion that this body signified. He said: "I would prefer to sacrifice everything than to cast aspersions on the integrity of Christ."

Teilhard's faith was scrupulously orthodox and was never threatened by the audacity of his new formulas or his attempts at reinterpretation. He asserted: "One can only be a Christian by absolutely and definitively believing in all the dogma. The least restriction on the extension or comprehension makes everything vanish."

Bruno de Solages, whose courageous friendship sustained Teilhard through difficult times, as did that of René d'Ouince and Henri de Lubac, explained Teilhard's point of view even further: "His preoccupation with conformity was constant and simultaneous with his concern about faithfulness to the Church. I remember a conversation in 1935 where we had together tossed around some very delicate dogmatic questions; he told me in conclusion: 'Happy are we with the authority of the Church! Left to ourselves, just how far would we drift away?'" (BDS, 341).

Henri de Lubac wrote: "About his entire work, we could say that it was the work of a believer who proposed his vision of Christ to humankind, a vision that was very personal, but a vision of the only Christ of the Gospel and of the Church." In this sense, Teilhard, whom we have, without sufficient reason—or even sometimes not having read him—reproached for attacking the foundations of the faith, will always be opposed to heretical tendencies and the risks of syncretism, of dissociation, or the dilution of the evangelical message. Thus, by comparing his own attitude with the modernist attitude, de Chardin could render this testimony: "The modernist 'volatilizes' Christ, dissociates him from the World. To the contrary, I seek to concentrate the World on Christ" (BDS, 342).

Teilhard's faith in the Church appears in the entirety of his work in two related forms—in his reformulations of the universal role of the Church and in his repeated and reasoned affirmations that results in the expression of a personal kerygma. This evangelizing message is a concentrated form of the basis of Teilhard's faith, and repeats his desire never to forsake the revealing axis of the Church. Furthermore, points out de Chardin: "Could God let those who strive to be 'pioneers'—those who humbly and without personal ambition love the Church and search for truth, those who have complete confidence in him and a preference for his divine will—could he let those separate themselves from him?" (GDP, 163).

Teilhard summed up his commitment this way: "The truth about the greatness of Christ is to be without limitations. Go ahead with all your heart and with all your intelligence, but don't separate yourself from the Christian trunk" (EP, 148).

As a convinced Catholic, Teilhard reaffirmed Rome's essential role, which for him represented—even if he made remarks about the central government of the Church—an essential pole of unity for the historical and mystical planes. Teilhard points out: "If Christianity is truly destined, like it professes and feels, to be the religion of tomorrow, it could only be by the living and organized axis of its Roman Catholicism that it could hope to measure up to the great modern human trends and make them its own" (X, 197).

The city of Rome where he would be convened—and which he would only consider with respect to the future, the past being only of secondary interest to him—left a strong impression on him. He wrote: "I am aware, it seems, of the extraordinary home of spiritual radiance built by two thousand years of history in this place; presently, it is truly here that I find the Christic pole of the earth to be; it is truly through here, I want to say, that the ascensional axis of humanization passes" (NLV, 294). He continues: "I have been impressed (and supported) by the extraordinary, truly imperturbable confidence of Christianity, in the immovability of its faith and truth" (NLV, 297).

This man, called to order by his superiors, who was living obedience as an act of love and the greatest communion with the risen Christ, this man who was subjected to questioning—at times in an unjust and cavalier manner—felt, inwardly and solidly, attached to the Christian trunk and to the Catholic tradition. We discover, with reference to this subject of faithfulness to Catholic dogma, certain astonishing passages about his interpretation of the dogma of infallibility. Teilhard wrote: "To say that the Church is infallible is to simply recognize that...the Christian group contains, within itself, and to a superior degree, the sense and the obscure potential which allows it to find, throughout innumerable gropings, its road all the way to maturity and fulfillment....Having said this, to locate, as the Catholics have done, the permanent organ of this phyletic infallibilty in the Councils—or by an even more advanced concentration of Christian conscience, in the Pope (by formulating and expressing not his own ideas, but the thoughts of the Church)—this could do nothing but conform to the great law of 'cephalization' which dominates all biological evolution" (X, 181).

For Teilhard, the Church is a great body in evolution. He used the term "phylum" (meaning an evolutionary series of forms) in order to describe the continuity of evolution in the Church. As Teilhard wrote: "The Mystical Body of Christ is alive, of him, through him, and with him; it continues to be not only a 'phylum' but a 'phylum of love'...inserted by God in the evolutionary process, the presence of the living which allows the Church to integrate the very movement of life into its continuity: the constant emergence of 'everything new'" (CUE, 197).

There is, in the Church, by reason of its close bonds with the risen Christ, a principle of development and evolution. Christianity that is lived in a specific spiritual and ritualistic tradition corresponds, however, with little effort, to the great transformation movement which affects the universe: "In this sense, Christ is in the Church as the sun is in our eyes. We see the same sun that our fathers did; however, we understand it in a more magnificent way. I believe that the Church is still a child. Christ, from whom it lives, is immeasurably greater than it can imagine, and yet in the thousands of years when the true face of Christ will be a little better uncovered, Christians from then will again recite the 'Credo' without hesitation" (XIII, 137).

In this Church, vocations are numerous and correspond to the multiplicity of the world in which God traces different, but convergent, roads. Says Teilhard: "There is an infinite number of vocations....In the Church, Saint Thomas of Aquinas and Saint Vincent de Paul sit next to Saint John of the Cross...but these different holinesses are nuances of the same spirit" (ER, 455). What vocations have in common is that they are signs of the holiness to which all men are called. Toward the end of his life, Teilhard often repeated what was lacking in the Church: "a new definition of holiness."

This must not be characterized by an escape from the world, but by a spiritual integration of reality in the steps to conversion and self-abandonment to Christ. He explains, in his *Short Introduction to Christianity*: "the 'Leave everything and follow me' of the Gospel only steers us toward 'everything' at a higher angle, as long as this 'everything' allows us to seize and prolong Christ in the reality of his Incarnation. No longer mortification above all, but the perfection of human effort, thanks to mortification" (X, 198).

In summary, de Chardin's definition of the Church sees it as the true place and center for the illumination of the world through the sanctifying grace of the living God.

REFLECTION QUESTIONS

Am I an active member of the Church, the Body of Christ? Do I recognize the value of the Church, its support in my seeking deeper relationship with God? Do I attempt to actively nurture and encourage other members of the Church as they seek deeper union with God?

BIBLE READING

The suggested Bible reading for meditation is 1 Peter 2:4–10.

PRAYER

You are our God and we are your people. Lead us, as a Church, toward the eternal sources. Amen.

DAY FOURTEEN
Wait and Hope

FOCUS POINT

As new members join its Body, the Church waits "in joyful hope for the coming of our Savior, Jesus Christ," all the while providing witness to his saving love and sacrifice. At the end of the world individuals will be left with the decision to adhere or to refuse the love of God and union with him.

Waiting...is the Christian function par excellence and perhaps the most distinctive trait of our religion. Historically, a period of waiting has never ceased to guide the progress of our faith like a beacon. The Israelites have been perpetual "waiters," as were the first Christians. Christmas, it seems, should have inversed the direction of our glances and concentrated them on the past, but it only directed them further ahead. During the brief time that Christ appeared among us, the Messiah only let himself be seen and touched so as to lose himself, more illuminating and more unutterable in the mists of the future.

But now we must wait for him again and anew....It is an accumulation of desires that will make the second coming of Christ at the end of time burst forth (IV, 197).

In Teilhard's mysticism, spiritual life culminates in a wait. The believer is focused toward the front, and all existence is marked by a profound dynamic of fulfillment. The destiny and the message of the one who said, "I have always lived ahead," could be easily compared to Advent, which comes before Christmas and is a celebration of God's sudden appearance in history and in all life. This time of Advent, at the beginning of winter, when everything is stripped bare, concentrates on the essential, with neither contrivance nor false security.

This Advent spirituality, by evoking the prophetic dimension of Christianity, suited Teilhard well. In him the constant attraction between the Incarnation and Resurrection was the source of this wait where Christ was the center. Wrote de Chardin, "Yes, Good Advent! All of Earth's activities...become a march toward the second coming of Christ at the end of time.... May the new Christmas unite us and unite all humankind in him, in a Christ that is always more clearly perceived at the center of the convergence of the world" (EP, 154, 157).

The world awaits, more often and in many ways, a Word and a message that equals the magnitude of questions asked. The wait is much more spiritual than material, qualitative than quantitative: "What Man awaits, at this moment," writes Father Pierre, "and what he dies not finding in things, is a complete food to nourish in him the passion to be more" (VII, 290).

But are we not too lukewarm or hesitant, too comfortable or bent on the past, too often nostalgic witnesses rather than innovators? Exclaims Teilhard: "Christians, only twenty centuries after the Ascension, having been given the responsibility, after Israel, to always keep the flame of desire alive on earth, what have we done about the wait?"

Christianity must, whatever it may cost, provide witness today of a trust and hope whose basis is none other than the very content of faith: the world, no matter what the bounds of its developments may be, is called to fulfillment in God. And that goal must mobilize our present energies.

Christ's triumph in no way abolishes man's interest, initiatives, or progress in the actual search: "We continually forget it. The supernatural is a ferment, a soul, not a complete organism. It comes to transform 'nature.' But it could never do without the matter that nature presents it....The wait for heaven could only live if it is incarnate. What body would we give to our own today—the one of a totally human and immense hope?" (IV, 199).

Our hope is not inhuman or superhuman, but totally human. Humanity is in a state of growth and the Universe's progressions are not in competition with God, no more than failure or death are opposed to him.

Faith is located at the crossroad of divine promises and human aspirations, but it does not place them in opposition to one another. All exclusionary points of view will be destructive to human and spiritual equilibrium. All suspicion brought on the world's progress will become a sign of unfaithfulness to the Word of God and to his creative breath. *The Divine Milieu* is fulfilled by these lines—certainly well known—on which we must take the time to meditate again:

> Why then, men of little faith, do you fear or pout over the progress of the world? Why do you carelessly multiply the prophesies and defenses: Don't go there....

Don't try it....Everything is known....The earth is empty and old....There is no longer anything to find.

Try everything for Christ! Hope everything for Christ!..."May nothing be condemned." That is the true Christian attitude. To deify is not to destroy but to supercreate. We will never know enough about what the Incarnation awaits from the powers of the world. We never have enough hope in growing human unity.

Lift up your head, Jerusalem. Look at the immense crowd of those who are building and of those who are seeking. In the laboratories, studios, deserts, factories, and in the enormous social melting pot, do you see all these people who are toiling? Well, all that ferments from them, their art, science, and thought, all of that is for you. Let us go. Open your arms, and your heart, as does your Lord Jesus and welcome the wave, the flood of human sap. Receive this sap, because without its baptism, you will disintegrate without desire, like a flower without water; and save them, until, without your sun, they will foolishly disperse on sterile stems.

Now, where is the temptation of the world which is too big, and the seduction of the world which is too beautiful? There is none.

Now the earth can embrace me with its giant arms. It can inflate me with its life or take me back into its dust. In my eyes, it can dress itself up with all its charms, horrors, or mysteries; it can throw me on my knees as I wait for what ripens in its womb.

Its charms cannot harm me, since for me it has become, way beyond itself, the Body of the One who is and the One to come! (IV, 201).

For Teilhard, the wait is also, and above all, an interior and secret activity. The wait must exist in a state of prayer and certain deprivation, away from noisy demonstrations or excessive statements. It shows the freedom of God at the center of the mystical experience. States de Chardin: "My soul, fold in your wings which you had spread wide open in order to reach the earthly summits where the light is brighter. And wait for fire to descend, if it wishes for you to be his" (XII, 186).

Interiority also determines hope. We will have indications of the road to follow if we can see: "In the conversion of the modern world, everything is a question of vision, everything must begin from an internal enlightenment....If the vision is there, the gift will come, almost infallibly. If men today are not giving of themselves, it is because they are not convinced by an appeal to their intelligence and heart" (EP, 148).

Let us not forget that the wait steers us toward the end, the ultimate, the Day of the Lord. What will it be? It is difficult to imagine. Vatican II tells us that we do not even have to imagine it. *Gaudium et Spes* says: "We do not know the time of the end of all time and humanity. We do not know the mode of transformation of the cosmos" (39:1). Also unknown is the manner in which the meeting will take place. Each meeting will be personal, since each one of us is unique in God's eyes. However, we must not forget this: "For God so loved the world that he gave his only Son, so that everyone who believes in him may not perish but have eternal life" (Jn 3:16). Salvation is a question of love, and it will come through Love.

Refusing to see fulfillment as a catastrophic end of the world, Teilhard believes that the final day will come upon a world which is at the point of extreme tension and freedom (the freedom to adhere or to refuse). And he concludes, in poetic and significant words, echoing Saint Luke's views (Lk 21:27) and those of Saint Paul (1 Cor 15:23): "Then, without a doubt, upon a creation pushed to the limits of its aptitudes for union, the glorious second coming of Christ will take place....The universal Christ will burst forth like a bolt of lightning amid the clouds of the slowly consecrated world." Individual destinies will then be fulfilled—"some...in the limitless achievement of an eternal Communion, others...in the conscious horrors of an endless decomposition." At that moment, Christ "will consume the universal unification by surrendering himself in his full adult Body... to the embraces of the Divinity...." And then the end will come. "Like a huge tide, the Being will have dominated the quivering of the creations. In the midst of a calmed ocean, of which each drop shall be conscious of remaining itself, the extraordinary adventure of the world will be finished....And God will be everything to everyone" (IX, 113).

REFLECTION QUESTION

Do I wait in joyous expectation of Christ's coming? Do I bear witness daily to the great love and sacrifice He shows me? Do I daily choose to follow Christ's example and adhere my will to his Divine Will?

BIBLE READING

The suggested Bible text for meditation is Revelation 21:1–6.

PRAYER

Lord Jesus, come, we are waiting for you. Awaken us and keep us attentive to the signs of the Kingdom. Amen.

DAY FIFTEEN

A Christianity of the Future

FOCUS POINT

For Teilhard, all the hopes and expectations of Christianity for the future are fulfilled by God through absolute faithfulness in him. The future is viewed with great optimism, as the world continues to evolve and grow toward God. It is through "panamorization," that is, transforming the world's structures by our love, that Christianity will retain its pivotal place in the world.

In fact, only Christianity remains standing today, able to measure up to the intellectual and moral world that exists in the West since the Renaissance....Christianity does not offer the opiate of a defeatist passivity, but the lucid rapture of a magnificent reality to be discovered by a push forward across the front of the Universe. In spite of some unavoidable awkwardness, Christianity has brought us up to this point...not nonhumans, but superhumans. That is why it remains acceptable, as a belief, for a generation which does not ask of religion to only keep us wise and to lick our wounds, but to make us critical, enthusiastic seekers and conquerors (XIII, 139).

In this last stop on our fifteen-day journey, we discuss one of the richest contributions of Teilhard's thinking and spirituality for our times. This concept is one of fundamental optimism (an expression of prophetic dimension that was dear to him). Teilhard, like John the Baptist, constantly strives to lift our gaze toward the One who never stops coming.

For Teilhard, the real strength of Christian faith is constituted in the proposition of spiritual, cultural, and social action, resulting from its source, the risen Christ. Christian faith provides an answer to the question of meaning, one still overly reserved to the elite, but which is continuously unfolding. He writes: "To me, it appears psychologically unavoidable that within two or three generations, humanity will be brought to collectively question itself about the meaning and value that it wants to have; and I have little doubt that the outcome will be an act of faith in the future....I believe that we are on the eve of passing through a critical point, beyond which only those who will do it religiously shall continue to search and build (that is, to live)" (EP, 110).

Today, we are living in unprecedented change, and Christianity clears a succession of thresholds just as does the humanity of which it is a part. It seems that, for Teilhard, in the twentieth century, Christianity will reach the limit of one of the natural cycles of its existence. He writes: "There is no sign left on earth of an expanding faith, but only of scattered, practically immobile credos; that is, when they are not clearly in regression...from there (and in spite of certain decisive, yet still underground symptoms of rebirth) comes this haunting impression of an increasing and irresistible de-Christianization" (V, 339).

Nevertheless, faced with great collective aspirations, nothing can bring us back to the past. Humanity has grown and we must band together with courage and faith in the face of this new situation. As early as 1916, Teilhard expressed the wish for a harmonizing synthesis of the natural and supernatural evolutions of humanity, writing: "The equilibrium of human development is not found in sole obedience to earthly laws, nor in the singular adhesion to the dogmas and to a spirit that has been revealed to us by the good Father that is in heaven, but it is found in an effort toward God that speeds up the blood through all the veins of humanity without exception" (XII, 88).

At first, the Church was wary and suspicious of a certain evolution of the world. Then, it engaged in an effort of difficult, yet necessary and irreversible, discernment. Today, many tasks appear to be a priority:

- First, to take note of an urgent problem: the great choices which humankind will be confronted with require a mobilization of all spiritual forces in the presence of, and amongst which, Christianity has a unique responsibility: "It gives an exact answer to the doubts and aspirations of an era that has been abruptly awakened and made conscious of its future. Christianity alone, in as much as we can judge, reveals itself able to justify and maintain the world's fundamental taste for life" (X, 112).
- To have confidence in man and be aware that, for Christians, the search for the absolute continues through the fulfillment and development of humanity.
- To make an unconditional commitment without mis-

taking humility for inconsistency. Teilhard writes: "We have already heard too much about lambs, I would like to hear about lions. Too much kindness and not enough strength. That is how I would symbolically summarize…the question of readjusting the evangelical doctrines to the modern world" (X, 109).

- To recall the profound meaning of the Incarnation. Our effort towards the realization of the world is defined by faith in one God. Says Father Pierre: "If the world was created for Christ, then all progress in this world makes man more apt to receive the Word of a God who is revealing his universal destiny to him."
- To realize a conversion which allows the birth of a new breed of Christians, so that Christianity can justify its claim when faced with contemporary knowledge. Teilhard comments: "May God give us and multiply those Christians who, by their religion, will bear, more than any other human, the weight of the aspirations and labors of their time….Without exaggerating, is there not a new cycle opening for the Church, a cycle that is marvellously adapted to the present age of Humanity? The cycle of Christ, adored throughout the universe. May those who hear the Master coming keep watch, desire and work…" (IX, 44).

The challenge may seem ambitious, but it is none other than the one that was accepted by the Second Vatican Council in modern times. Teilhard's appeal retains its pertinence, even if, over the last quarter of a century, the perspectives have changed, going from a conception of progress that was too radically optimistic to a more realistic and modest approach with respect to the new threats that characterize our time.

For Teilhard, the term "Christianity of the future" means nothing more than "absolute faithfulness" to the God of origins who alone can meet the expectations of humanity. Suspected of venturing into "a Christianity that has nothing left to do with tradition," Teilhard explains: "The universal Christ who satisfies my personal faith is nothing more than the authentic expression of the Christ of the Gospel....I have been accused of being an innovator. In truth, the more I have meditated on the magnificent cosmic attributes given by Saint Paul to the risen Christ...the more I have become aware that Christianity only took on its full value when brought (as I like to do) to universal dimensions" (X, 149).

By nature, Teilhard is, at all times, the man of the "new era," a man of tomorrow, a witness to the future, without ever ceasing to uncover and manifest the profound unity that characterizes all of Revelation. Is that where his stature as a visionary and prophet is revealed? He broaches that question in 1919 in his *Notes for the Evangelization of a New Era*, an essential text that is too seldom cited. God and history can be neither dissociated nor in conflict. Points out de Chardin: "The God that our century awaits must be (1) As vast and mysterious as the cosmos; (2) As immediate and enveloping as life; and (3) As linked to our effort as to our humanity" (XII, 401).

Christian faith is less and less visible in a world which, nevertheless, has never produced so many essays and research projects. The most serious threat to Christian faith, in Teilhard's eyes, is a rupture within reality itself, the separation of the evangelical ideal from man's long quest.

However, in the face of this quest, Christianity, "far from losing its dominance over the vast religious collective which is set loose by the modern world's totalization, to the contrary, it retains and consolidates its pivotal place...as long as sufficient attention is given to its extraordinary and significant power of panamorization." (Teilhard means by this word the capacity to transform, through love, all of the world's structures.)

In his last text, *The Christic*, which we can, in essence, consider to be his last will and testament, Teilhard, feeling the end near (the text was only finished a month before his death), confirms his confidence in his view of a Christianity that is perfectly adapted to the human quest: "I repeat, Christianity, again and forever, is but a 'reborn' Christianity...singularly able (through its double virtue of the Cross and Resurrection) to become the religion, which specifically drives evolution" (XIII, 114).

In spite of the legitimate doubts—signs of his profound intellectual and spiritual sincerity—which marked Teilhard's final days, certainty prevailed. Simply because, according to his very last words which we could inscribe on the forehead of our fate as his final legacy: "It is enough for truth to appear just once in only one mind in order that nothing can ever prevent it from invading and igniting everything" (XIII, 117).

REFLECTION QUESTIONS

Am I optimistic about the future? Am I confident in the development of humanity, as it seeks fulfillment in its search for the absolute? Am I optimistic that my own faith in God will bear fruit in my life—through loving action for my fellow brothers and sisters?

BIBLE READING

The suggested Bible passage for meditation is Luke 24:13–50.

PRAYER

O Holy Spirit, send us on the roads of the world to be witnesses of peace and hope. Amen.

Conclusion

"He Gave the Impression of Being Saved"

AT FATHER TEILHARD DE CHARDIN'S memorial service on April 27, 1955, in France, Father d'Ouince, who had been his Provincial and friend, said the following words: "He was a witness to the victory of Jesus Christ. He irresistibly gave the impression of being saved...."

How could we conclude a journey in prayer with Teilhard if not by evoking those words which warrant, on their own, a long demonstration? The risen Christ was, throughout Teilhard's life, the source and the horizon of his faith, of his determination and of his courage.

This man who enjoyed innumerable talents and a superior intellect was, in fact, a model of humility through his total openness to the mystery of God and his adhesion to Christ. He never ceased to be a disciple through his constant prayer, and even through the risk he took in his research and his intuitive thinking.

He was passionate for the cause of humankind, but a humankind that was made by God's liberating breath and turned toward God, like a ray of light.

He was passionate for the cause of the world, the abysses and the summits of the world which would become, in spite of death and suffering, places where the greatest hope possible exists.

He was passionate for the interior causes of beings and things. Man seemed to have understood these interior causes in spite of all the limits imposed on him, knowing that the human spirit hides such a power of unity and love that nothing can prevent the universal destiny from coming to fruition in God, in the flames of a definitive peace.

To reflect with Teilhard is to open oneself to the widest perspectives and to the strongest changes of our times, without the fear of anyone or anything.

To pray with Teilhard is to permanently get closer to the living source. It is to receive a Word that gives life, that brings rebirth, that supports and turns towards the future, through the strength of the Spirit—a Word which gathers and guides each of us to our fulfillment.

Teilhard systematically spoke little of prayer, but he had lived a life of prayer, and we progressively discover that nothing would have been taught and written had there not been, first and foremost, that extraordinary experience of a God who transforms everything.

A life is like a tree stretched between waiting and fulfillment.

The calls have been sent, and the cry echoed by a thousand civilizations that keeps being planted in our flesh and our hearts.

Happy are those who can see....Those hear beyond the pitfalls of our contradictions.

Happy are those who distinguish the light and the fundamental hope. For they will help us to rise up beyond the summit to understand that the universal dawn is seeded by the freedom of the Cross.

Bibliography

Anderson, Irvine H. *History in a Teilhardian Context: The Thought of Teilhard de Chardin As a Guide to Social Science.* (Teilhard Studies: No. 17). 1987.

Baltazar, Eulalio. *Liberation Theology & Teilhard de Chardin.* (Teilhard Studies: No. 20). 1989.

Birx, H. James. *Interpreting Evolution: Darwin & Teilhard de Chardin.* Prometheus Books. 1971.

Bruteau, Beatrice. *Evolution Toward Divinity: Teilhard de Chardin and the Hindu Traditions.* Theosophical Publishing House. 1974.

Faricy, Robert S. *The Spirituality of Teilhard de Chardin.* Harper SF. 1981.

Gray, Donald P. *A New Creation Story: The Creative Spirituality of Teilhard de Chardin.* (Teilhard Studies: No. 2). 1979.

Grim, John A. and Mary E. Grim. *Teilhard de Chardin: A Short Biography.* (Teilhard Studies, No. 11). 1984.

Hale, Robert F. *Christ and the Universe: Teilhard de Chardin and the Cosmos.* Chicago: Franciscan Herald Press. 1973.

Kessler, Marvin and Bernard Brown, eds. *Dimensions of the Future: The Spirituality of Teilhard de Chardin.* Washington: Corpus Books. 1968.

King, Ursula. *Christ in All Things: Exploring Spirituality with Teilhard de Chardin.* Orbis Books. 1997.

___. *Spirit of Fire: The Life and Vision of Teilhard de Chardin.* Orbis Books. 1998.

Lane, David. *The Phenomenon of Teilhard: Prophet for a New Age.* Mercer University Press. 1996.

Overzee, Anne Hunt. *The Body Divine: The Symbol of the Body in the Works of Teilhard de Chardin and Ramanuja.* Cambridge University Press. 1992.

Simon, Charlie May Hogue. *Faith Has Need of All the Truth: A Life of Pierre Teilhard de Chardin.* New York: Dutton. 1974.

Teilhard de Chardin, Pierre. *Christianity & Evolution.* Harcourt Brace. 1974.

___. *The Divine Milieu: An Essay on the Interior Life.* HarperCollins. 1975.

___. *Phenomenon of Man.* HarperCollins. 1975.

___. *Toward the Future.* Harcourt Brace. 1975.

___. *Building the Earth.* London: Chapman. 1965.

___. *Meditations with Teilhard de Chardin.* Santa Fe, N.M.: Bear. 1988.

___. *On Love & Happiness.* San Francisco: Harper & Row. 1984.

___. *Science and Christ.* New York: Harper & Row. 1968.

___. *On Suffering.* New York: Harper & Row. 1974.

___. *On Happiness.* London: Collins. 1973.

Tucker, Mary E. *The Ecological Spirituality of Teilhard.* (Teilhard Studies: No. 13). 1985.